Ridgewood Grammar

THE LANGUAGE CONNECTION

BOOK TWO

Nancy Bison and Terri Wiss

EDUCATORS PUBLISHING SERVICE
Cambridge and Toronto

Cover and interior design by Joni Doherty

Printed in USA

ISBN 978-0-8388-2393-4

10 11 PPG 13

CONTENTS

INTRODUCTION

What is grammar? Why is it important?

Grammar is a set of rules for speaking and writing. It helps everyone speak, read, and write, just as the rules for a game help everyone understand how to play. Grammar gives names or labels to specific parts of the English language, and it tells us how to use them. It labels words and groups of words.

In our daily life, we need to know the names for things and how those things are used. For example, if you look around your kitchen, you see a refrigerator and a stove. You know that you use the refrigerator to keep food cold. You use the stove to cook food. Using this book will help you learn grammar—what the names for some words are and how they work. Knowing the rules of grammar will help you use language. You will become a better speaker, reader, and writer. You will express your thoughts clearly. Your writing will be easier to follow. You will read with more understanding. Grammar is an important part of your education. We hope you enjoy learning it.

THE BASICS

Language is made up of different parts that work together to help people express their ideas. An idea is often expressed as a **sentence,** which is a group of words that contains a subject and a verb; a sentence expresses a complete thought.

Read the following sentences:

Annie saw a helicopter.
Tomorrow I am going to the movies.
This recipe seems complicated.

The **subject** tells you what person, place, object/thing, idea, or feeling is involved; the **verb** either tells you what the subject is doing or tells you about the subject's condition. *Annie, I,* and *recipe* are all subjects. *Saw, am going,* and *seems* are all verbs. As you work in this book, you will learn more about subjects, verbs, and sentences. Knowing about these parts of language will help you communicate better.

EXERCISE 1

In the sentences below, circle the subject and underline the verb. The first one is done for you.

1. (Jamal) <u>likes</u> skateboarding better than in-line skating.

✓2. Last weekend (I) <u>baked</u> bread.

✓ 3. This (book) <u>looks</u> easy to read.

✓4. (Zebras) <u>are</u> Kate's favorite animal.

✓5. (I) <u>will visit</u> Aunt Rebecca this weekend.

✓6. (Celine) <u>passed</u> the test.

✓ 7. (Ian) <u>eats</u> an apple every day.

EXERCISE 2

Now write your own sentences, using the subjects and verbs below. Your sentences can be serious or silly.

SUBJECTS	VERBS
hippopotamus	play
Christine	laugh
monkey	break
racecar	spin

The hippopotamus breaks Christine.

The monkey will play.

Her racecar will spin out.

SENTENCES

ABOUT SENTENCES

Although we don't always speak in complete sentences, we should usually construct complete sentences when we write. Complete sentences have a **subject** and a **verb.** They help those who read our writing understand our thoughts and ideas. Complete sentences also help writers to clearly state thoughts or questions. Good writers try to write exactly what they mean.

Sentences have a structure that includes a **subject** and a **predicate.** A **complete subject** tells who or what the sentence is about. It can be one word or more than one word. A complete predicate contains the verb and other information about the subject. Look at the sentences below.

> Many people love baseball.
> Computers play an important role in our lives.
> Science experiments are the most fun!

In the first sentence the subject is *Many people*. The predicate is *love baseball*, and the verb is *love*. The parts of the sentence can be shown like this:

COMPLETE SUBJECT	COMPLETE PREDICATE
Many people	love baseball.

Notice how the predicate, *love baseball*, tells something about the subject, *Many people*.

In the second sentence the subject is *Computers*. The predicate is *play an important role in our lives*, and the verb is *play*. The parts of that sentence can be shown the same way:

COMPLETE SUBJECT   COMPLETE PREDICATE

Computers | play an important role in our lives.

Again, the predicate, *play an important role in our lives*, tells something about the subject, *Computers*.

In the third sentence the subject is *Science experiments*. The predicate is *are the most fun*, and the verb is *are*. Show how the parts of the sentence should be written on the line below:

COMPLETE SUBJECT   COMPLETE PREDICATE

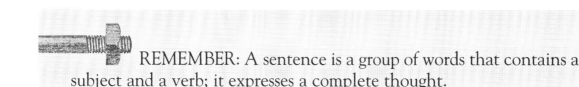

What does the predicate tell you about the subject?

_____

There are two types of verbs used in sentences. One type is called **action verbs.** *Play* and *love* are action verbs. The other type is called **linking verbs.** In the third sentence above, *are* is a linking verb. Whether action verbs show physical action like *play* or mental action like *love*, action verbs tell what is happening. Linking verbs, on the other hand, connect the subject to the rest of the sentence (the predicate).

REMEMBER: A sentence is a group of words that contains a subject and a verb; it expresses a complete thought.

EXERCISE 1

In the sentences below, underline the complete subject once. Underline the complete predicate twice. Draw a vertical line (|) between the subject and predicate. The first one is done for you.

1. Chilly weather | came early this year.

2. I noticed cool evenings first.

3. Leaves changed colors.

4. A few leaves fell from trees.

5. It gets dark early now.

6. Squirrels collect acorns for the winter.

7. Flocks of birds fly south.

8. The market sells apple cider.

9. Pumpkins decorate many homes.

10. It will be Halloween soon!

EXERCISE 2

In the chart below the following sentences, write the complete subject and complete predicate in the correct place. The first one is done for you.

1. Mr. Jackson assigned a report on leaves.

2. Students will collect different types.

3. They will identify the leaves by name.

4. Rebecca pasted her leaves on construction paper.

5. She labeled them with colored ink.

6. Jill worked with Rebecca.

7. Jill's father knows a great deal about trees.

8. He told the girls unusual facts.

9. They looked in books for more information.

10. Mr. Jackson said their report was excellent!

COMPLETE SUBJECT	COMPLETE PREDICATE
1. Mr. Jackson	assigned a report on leaves.
2.	

COMPLETE SUBJECT	COMPLETE PREDICATE
3. _____	_____
4. _____	_____
5. _____	_____
6. _____	_____
7. _____	_____
8. _____	_____
9. _____	_____
10. _____	_____

SIMPLE SUBJECTS

A **complete subject** is what is being talked about in the sentence. It can be one word or more than one word. When a complete subject is more than one word, usually one of the words is more important than the others. It will be the main word or name in the complete subject. It is called the **simple subject.** Sometimes the simple subject and the complete subject are the same.

Look again at the sentences that introduced the complete subject and complete predicate. Here the simple subjects are underlined:

Many <u>people</u> love baseball.
<u>Computers</u> play an important role in our lives.
Science <u>experiments</u> are the most fun!

In the next group of sentences, the simple subjects are names of people, places, and things.

Thanksgiving is a time for family gatherings.
Dr. Martin Luther King Jr. believed in equality.
The Colorado River winds through the Grand Canyon.
The mighty Hudson River divides New York and New Jersey.

REMEMBER: A simple subject is the main word or name in the complete subject that tells exactly what is being talked about in the sentence. (It can be more than one word or name.)

EXERCISE 1

In the following sentences, underline the simple subject. The first one is done for you.

1. Christa McAuliffe School teaches research skills in all the grades.

2. Students learn to gather information from many sources.

3. CD-ROM encyclopedias make research faster.

4. The library contains books on specific subjects.

5. The upper grade teachers have some materials in their classrooms.

6. Students learn about primary sources.

7. They practice interviewing skills.

8. Certain television programs provide data.

9. Note-taking lessons become very important.

10. Some research skills are more difficult to learn than others.

EXERCISE 2

In the following sentences, underline the simple subject. Then use that simple subject to write a sentence of your own on the line provided. The first one is done for you.

1. The upper grade <u>students</u> produced a living museum.

   Students play ball after school.

2. Everyone pretended to be a famous person in history.

3. The teachers chose the characters.

4. The girl playing Harriet Tubman gave the most compelling speech.

5. The living museum was a huge success.

SIMPLE PREDICATES

A complete predicate contains the verb and other information about the subject. The **simple predicate** is always the verb that shows the action or links the subject to the rest of the sentence. It is the main word or words in the complete predicate.

In the sentences below, the simple predicates are underlined.

Many people <u>love</u> baseball.
Computers <u>play</u> an important role in our lives.
Science experiments <u>are</u> the most fun!
Thanksgiving <u>is</u> a time for family gatherings.
Dr. Martin Luther King Jr. <u>believed</u> in equality.

The Colorado River <u>winds</u> through the Grand Canyon.
The mighty Hudson River <u>divides</u> New York and New Jersey.

Notice that each simple predicate tells something about its subject.

 REMEMBER: The simple predicate is always a verb.

EXERCISE 1

In the following sentences, underline the simple predicate. The first one is done for you.

1. The sixth graders <u>learned</u> about fire during science.

2. Fire produces heat and light.

3. The students asked many questions.

4. Glowing particles form flames.

5. Three conditions are necessary for fire: oxygen, heat, and fuel.

6. Air provides oxygen.

7. The high temperature is called the ignition temperature.

8. Wood and paper are two kinds of fuel.

9. The teacher explained the word *combustible*.

10. *Combustible* means capable of catching fire and burning.

EXERCISE 2

In the following sentences, underline the simple predicate. Then use the simple predicate in a sentence of your own on the line provided. The first one is done for you.

1. The main ingredients of chewing gum <u>are</u> sweetener, flavor, and gum base.

Grapes are my favorite fruit.

2. Gum base keeps gum chewy for hours.

_____

3. Bubble gum will stretch the most.

_____

4. Some popular flavors are spearmint, peppermint, and cinnamon.

_____

5. Each manufacturer guards a secret recipe.

_____

6. Powdered sugar prevents the gum from sticking.

_____

7. Knives cut ribbons of gum into sticks.

_____

8. Machines wrap the sticks separately.

_____

SENTENCE FRAGMENTS

Some groups of words appear to be sentences but are not. When a group of words does not have a complete thought, it is not truly a sentence. It is a **sentence fragment.** _Fragment_ means _part_. A sentence fragment is missing either a subject or a predicate.

Here are some examples of sentence fragments missing predicates:

The exciting movie in town.
The geraniums on the windowsill.
Early in the morning the robins.

Here are some examples of sentence fragments missing subjects:

Drew large crowds.
Wilted in the hot sun.
Gave their daily concert.

The subject fragments and the predicate fragments in the examples above could be combined to form complete sentences.

COMPLETE SUBJECT	COMPLETE PREDICATE
The exciting movie in town	drew large crowds.
The geraniums on the windowsill	wilted in the hot sun.
Early in the morning the robins	gave their daily concert.

Most people use sentence fragments when they speak. If someone asked you, "What's your favorite book?" you probably would not say, "My favorite book is *Bridge to Terabithia*." You would probably just say the title of the book. But when you write, you should use complete sentences so that your readers will be sure to understand you.

EXERCISE 1

Read the groups of words below. Write *sentence* on the line if the words form a complete thought. Write *fragment* on the line if the words do not form a complete thought. The first one is done for you.

fragment _____ 1. The physical education teachers at our school.

_____ 2. The town Olympics were planned for the spring.

_____ 3. Always placed in the top three.

_____ 4. The four-person medley is an exciting event.

_____ 5. Runners in the international Olympics set high

standards for school athletes.

_____ 6. Data on the computer.

_____ 7. The spirit of the Olympics.

_____ 8. Our school has an outstanding sixth grade runner.

_____ 9. Moved here from Australia last year.

_____ 10. Early morning tryouts for the teams.

EXERCISE 2

Create complete sentences from the groups of words below by adding a subject or a predicate. Write the completed sentence on the line; then tell whether you added a subject or predicate by circling the appropriate word. The first one is done for you.

1. my best friend and I

   My best friend and I asked the new girl on our block to play goalie.

   Subject / (Predicate)

2. the glowing full moon

   _____

   Subject / Predicate

3. spoke to his grandparents in Korea

   _____

   Subject / Predicate

4. played charades at the drama club meeting

   _____

   Subject / Predicate

5. quickly jumped out of the way

_____

Subject / Predicate

6. Mr. Belachek, the art teacher

_____

Subject / Predicate

7. began a peer tutoring program

_____

Subject / Predicate

8. a famous teenage actor

_____

Subject / Predicate

SENTENCE DIAGRAMMING USING GRAPHIC ORGANIZERS

This section shows how to diagram the most important words in a sentence. A sentence diagram is a type of graphic organizer. *Graphic* means "having to do with pictures." Graphic organizers help you arrange or present information as a picture. In this case, a sentence diagram is an organized picture that shows what the words in a sentence do. This book will use the terms *graphic organizer* and *sentence diagram* to refer to the same thing.

Diagrams begin with the simple subject and the simple predicate. They are the most important words in a sentence. As you work through this book, you will learn how to diagram other words.

Diagramming Simple Subjects and Simple Predicates

The simple subject and simple predicate are written on a horizontal line (_____). They are separated from each other by a vertical or up-and-down line (|) that intersects or cuts through the horizontal line. We have already seen these diagrams earlier in this book.

Look at the sentence below.

Raindrops glisten.

The simple subject is *Raindrops*. The simple predicate or verb is *glisten*. They are diagrammed as follows:

| raindrops | glisten |

Notice that there is no punctuation in a diagram.
Look at the next sentence.

The falling hail tapped against the window.

The simple subject is *hail*. The simple predicate or verb is *tapped*. They are diagrammed as follows:

| hail | tapped |

EXERCISE 1

Place the simple subjects and simple predicates from the sentences below in the diagrams provided. The first one is done for you.

1. Leaves fell.

| leaves | fell |

2. Cats purred.

3. Dad cooks.

4. The plane arrived late.

5. The minutes ticked away slowly.

6. The students ran to the climbing wall.

7. Multicolored confetti covered the floor.

8. We watched a video about life in the desert.

EXERCISE 2

In the following sentences, draw the diagrams yourself. Write the simple subject before the vertical line. Write the simple predicate after the vertical line. Use a ruler to help you make straight lines.

1. Many grandparents attended Grandparents' Day.

2. Casey locked her bicycle on the bike rack.

3. Seven students competed in the first-level gymnastics meet.

4. Our town has two libraries.

5. Dr. Ruiz examined my throat.

FOUR TYPES OF SENTENCES

There are four kinds of sentences: declarative, interrogative, imperative, and exclamatory. Each one has its own pattern and does a different job.

A **declarative sentence** tells something. This type of sentence ends with a period (.). Declarative sentences usually have the format you've learned: complete subject | complete predicate. A declarative sentence is sometimes called a **statement.**

The sun	rises in the east and sets in the west.
The earth	rotates on its axis.
The moon	orbits the earth.

An **interrogative sentence** asks a question. This type of sentence ends with a question mark (?). This type of sentence can begin with *who, what, when, where, why,* or *how,* or it can begin with a verb. An interrogative sentence is usually called a **question.**

Where does the sun set?
Does the earth rotate on its axis?
Does the moon orbit the earth?

An **imperative sentence** gives a command or makes a request and usually ends with a period (.). The **command** is a firm order. This kind of sentence usually begins with a verb that does the ordering. The **request** is a type of command that uses more polite language. It typically begins with *please* or *kindly.*

COMMANDS

Take your shoes off at the door.
Write your name on the line.
Line up quietly when there is a fire drill.

REQUESTS

Please turn off the light.
Kindly return this book to the library.
Please choose your topic carefully.

An **exclamatory sentence** shows surprise, excitement, fear, or some other strong or sudden feeling. It ends with an exclamation point (!). The exclamatory sentence is sometimes called an **exclamation.** This type of sentence may begin in a variety of ways. It is the strong emotion that determines its type.

Ouch, that hurts!
Run for your life!
This is a scary movie!

EXERCISE 1

Identify each sentence by writing *declarative, interrogative, imperative,* or *exclamatory* on the line before each sentence.

1. _____ Mrs. McDonough brought Kelly to the doctor for a checkup.

2. _____ Dr. Ruiz tapped Kelly's knee with a small rubber hammer.

3. _____ Kelly almost kicked the doctor!

4. _____ Dr. Ruiz knew she didn't mean to kick him.

5. _____ He explained that the kick was a reflex action.

6. _____ "What causes a reflex action?"

7. _____ "A reflex action is an automatic response that the body makes."

8. _____ Name two actions that are automatic.

9. _____ Can you control an act that is not voluntary?

10. _____ I wish I could control the hiccups!

11. _____ Blink your eye if a speck of dust flies in it.

12. _____ Over 90 percent of our actions are reflexes!

RIDGEWOOD GRAMMAR

EXERCISE 2

Punctuate the following sentences by placing a period, question mark, or exclamation point on the line at the end of the sentence.

1. How fast does hair grow _____

2. Hair grows about half an inch a month _____

3. Did you know the speed of growth varies with the time of day _____

4. At night hair grows slowly, but it speeds up during the day _____

5. Take good care of your hair _____

6. People have different amounts _____

7. Imagine hair several feet long _____

8. Keep your scalp clean _____

9. Hair conserves the heat in your body _____

10. I love bright red hair _____

EXERCISE 3

On the lines below, write a sentence of your own that fits each type.

1. Declarative

_____

2. Interrogative

_____

3. Imperative (command)

_____

4. Imperative (request)

_____

5. Exclamatory

_____

SENTENCE REVIEW EXERCISES

 REMEMBER: A sentence is a group of words that express a complete thought. It has a complete subject that tells what is being talked about in the sentence. It has a complete predicate that contains a verb and other information about the subject.

EXERCISE 1

In each of the following sentences, underline the complete subject once, underline the complete predicate twice, and draw a vertical line (|) to separate the subject from the predicate.

1. Students are preparing for student government elections.

2. Seven teams of candidates are running this year.

3. Each team has candidates for president, vice-president, secretary, and treasurer.

4. The teams hang posters on the bulletin boards in the hallways.

5. The posters tell about the candidates and their promises and hopes for the school.

6. Each presidential candidate speaks at an assembly of students from fourth through eighth grade.

7. Those students vote the next day.

8. The principal and her secretary count the ballots.

9. The winning team is announced at the end of the school day.

10. The officers are sworn in the following morning in the auditorium.

EXERCISE 2

Read the following paragraphs. Then go back and underline the <u>complete subject</u> once, underline the <u>complete predicate</u> twice, and draw a vertical line (|) to separate the subject from the predicate.

Fairy tales are a type of folktale. Literature scholars prefer to call fairy tales by their German name, Marchen. Two of the most famous collectors of Marchen were German. Their names were Jakob and Wilhelm Grimm. Their most well-known collection is called *Grimm's Fairy Tales.*

Grimm's Fairy Tales is a collection of imaginative stories filled with unbelievable events. A hero or heroine is usually the main character. This character goes through difficult times. He or she often performs tasks that seem impossible. Someone or something usually provides help just in time. This helper is often magical. Some of these stories end with the words "and they lived happily ever after."

Marchen are part of the history of literature. These tales have passed from one generation to another by word of mouth. Actors or storytellers have performed these stories for centuries. Most people could not read long ago. Fairy tales now can be read in books or viewed on video. Actors still sometimes perform fairy tales. Professional storytellers present them, too. It is fun and different to see a favorite story acted out. Both young people and adults enjoy Marchen. Jakob and Wilhelm Grimm helped preserve a folk tradition.

EXERCISE 3

Rewrite a favorite fairy tale in your own words on the lines below. Be sure to write in complete sentences. Capitalize and punctuate each sentence.

_____

_____

_____

_____

_____

_____

_____

_____

_____

REMEMBER: A simple subject is the main word or name in the complete subject. It is what is being talked about in the sentence. (It can be more than one word or name.)

EXERCISE 4

In the following sentences, underline the simple subject.

1. Pure water is an odorless and tasteless liquid.

2. The freezing point of water is 32 degrees Fahrenheit.

3. It boils at 212 degrees Fahrenheit.

4. This liquid expands upon freezing.

5. Water is called a compound.

6. H_2O is the scientific name of this compound.

7. This substance is a combination of hydrogen and oxygen.

8. Water can be found as a solid, a liquid, or a gas.

EXERCISE 5

Use the words below as simple subjects in sentences of your own. Underline the simple subjects.

1. fog

_____

2. steam

_____

3. water

_____

4. liquid

_____

5. ice

_____

REMEMBER: The simple predicate can be defined as the main word or words in the complete predicate. The simple predicate is always a verb.

EXERCISE 6

Underline the simple predicate in each of the sentences below.

1. Some of the classes were singing "Puff, the Magic Dragon" in music.

2. They asked the music teacher questions about dragons.

3. She answered their questions.

4. Then she told them several legends and myths.

5. Dragons were legendary monsters with wings and a fiery breath.

6. They usually represented evil.

7. Dragons were good creatures in some stories, though.

8. The ancient Greeks believed good things about dragons.

9. Some soldiers of ancient Rome carried flags with pictures of dragons.

10. The ancient sailors of Scandinavia carved dragons on the front of their boats.

EXERCISE 7

Use the following verbs as simple predicates in sentences of your own. Then underline the simple predicate in each sentence.

1. try

_____

2. had written

_____

3. was pitching

_____

RIDGEWOOD GRAMMAR

4. studied

_____

5. is counting

_____

6. dreamed

_____

7. skates

_____

8. discuss

_____

REMEMBER: When a group of words does not express a complete thought, it is not a sentence. It is only part of a sentence, a fragment.

EXERCISE 8

Read the groups of words below. If the words form a sentence, draw a vertical line (|) between the complete subject and the complete predicate. If the words do not form a sentence, rewrite them and add the missing part. Then draw a vertical line between the complete subject and the complete predicate.

1. Reading is a way to learn about the world.

_____

2. It can also be fun.

_____

3. Sometimes before bedtime.

_____

4. Young children love fairy tales.

_____

5. Like them, too.

_____

6. Some children learn to read before they go to kindergarten.

_____

7. Reads to his class every day.

_____

8. A world without books.

_____

Read the paragraph below for content and meaning; then decide which groups of words are not sentences. In the space above the sentences, write a subject, predicate, or both for each fragment. Then rewrite the entire paragraph on the lines provided. Be sure to capitalize the first word in each sentence.

On Saturday I went to Water World with my dad. We saw many exhibits and shows. But we did not see every exhibit. We got to the aquarium at 10 A.M. We went to the dolphin show. Because we were too late for the killer whale show. Dad liked the rainforest on the top floor of the aquarium. It was hot and humid up there. Not like the rest of the aquarium. I saw a bright green snake and a tiny orange frog on a tree. After we ate lunch. I can't wait to go back to Water World! Maybe next year.

_____

_____

_____

_____

_____

_____

_____

_____

_____

_____

REMEMBER: A diagram is an organized picture of the words in a sentence that shows what the words do. It begins with two basic lines, the horizontal line (_____) and the vertical line (|) that intersects it.

EXERCISE 10

Place the simple subjects and the simple predicates in the diagrams provided.

1. Engines roared.

2. The teacher spoke softly.

3. The movie ended early.

4. Mrs. Mason polished her daughter's nails before the party.

5. Tyler's grandparents arrived just after breakfast.

RIDGEWOOD GRAMMAR

Place the simple subjects and the simple predicates from the following sentences in diagrams that you draw yourself. Use a ruler for neatness.

1. The ice cream melted.

2. People of all ages love the circus.

3. The main character of my short story has an active imagination.

4. The Internet has changed the lives of people all over the world.

5. Ms. Buchanan switches line leaders every week.

REMEMBER: A declarative sentence tells something. It ends with a period. An interrogative sentence asks a question. It ends with a question mark. An imperative sentence gives a command or makes a request. It usually ends with a period. An exclamatory sentence shows surprise, excitement, fear, or another strong or sudden feeling. It ends with an exclamation point.

EXERCISE 12

Identify each sentence by writing declarative, interrogative, imperative, or exclamatory on the line before each sentence.

1. _____ Oops, I tripped!

2. _____ What is the correct time?

3. _____ The school bus arrived at the museum on time.

4. _____ Where did you leave your bike?

5. _____ Take an umbrella with you.

6. _____ I'm scared!

7. _____ Most of the students eat lunch at school.

8. _____ Whisper, please.

EXERCISE 13

Write a sentence of your own that fits each type named.

1. Exclamatory

_____

2. Request

_____

3. Declarative

_____

4. Interrogative

_____

5. Command

_____

VERBS

ABOUT ACTION VERBS

Read the following passage:

Lila and Adele **decide** to see a movie. First they **discuss** the different movies at the nearby theater. Lila **votes** for the one about dinosaurs. She **thinks** they will love it. Then they **call** the theater for showtimes. They **ride** to the theater and **lock** their bicycles to the rack. Adele **buys** popcorn and **shares** it with Lila. They **talk** quietly until the start of the movie.

The words in bold print are called **verbs**. These words are the most important words in a sentence. In the sentences above, the verbs show action. They show that people decide, discuss, vote, think, love, call, bike, lock, buy, share, and talk.

Some actions are physical like *discuss* and *call*. Some actions are mental like *decide* and *think*. Whether they show physical or mental action, action verbs tell you what is happening. Just as an engine powers a car, a verb powers a sentence.

Action verbs are the building blocks of sentences. They help move thoughts along. They enliven conversation and writing by telling or showing exactly what the action is.

Verbs also connect the subject of the sentence to the rest of the sentence. Subjects tell who or what is doing the action the verb describes. Without the subject the action of the verb has no meaning.

Here are some examples:

SUBJECT	VERB	THE REST OF THE SENTENCE
The students	practiced	the new school song.
Tisha and Lori	walk	to school every day.
Ms. Buchanan	had taught	in Dallas before she came here.

In the following sentences there is a vertical line separating the subject and the predicate. As you can see, the complete subject of the first sentence is *The students*.

"The students | practiced" is the subject | verb in the first sentence.

"Tisha and Lori | walk" is the subject | verb in the second one.

"Ms. Buchanan | had taught" is the subject | verb in the third.

In speech or writing, every verb must have a subject.

EXERCISE 1

Underline each action verb that tells about its subject.

1. The students laughed at Mr. Williams' jokes.

2. Amahl sewed a button on his shirt.

3. Rebecca's younger sister believes in the Tooth Fairy.

4. Chanda and Alyson visited Mrs. Janssen, their third-grade teacher.

5. The students looked at drops of pond water through the microscope.

6. The teachers decorated the halls for the opening day of school.

7. Ms. Fernandez, the principal, rang the alarm for the fire drill.

8. Colette and Tami sometimes ride their bikes to school.

9. Ms. Buchanan announced a science test on Friday.

10. Her students groaned.

EXERCISE 2

Fill in the following chart with the parts of the sentences below. The first one is done for you.

1. Molly and Keesha talk on the phone every day.

2. Most of my classmates enjoy school.

3. Mr. Dunn told the children about his summer trip to Oregon.

4. Mike's parents bought concert tickets.

5. The teachers planned the first field trip.

6. Ms. Buchanan praised Anna's artwork.

7. Colin travels with his family on school vacations.

8. The new school nurse smiled at us.

	SUBJECT	VERB	THE REST OF THE SENTENCE
1.	Molly and Keesha	talk	on the phone every day.
2.			
3.			
4.			
5.			
6.			
7.			
8.			

EXERCISE 3

Write action verbs for the following subjects.

1. The athletes _____.

2. My grandmother _____.

3. Her best friend _____.

4. Some of the boys _____.

5. Geoff's relatives _____.

6. Rachel and Hope _____.

7. The team members _____.

8. The visiting author _____.

EXERCISE 4

Some action verbs express or show physical movement like *run* and *dance*. Some action verbs express or show mental action like *think* and *believe*. In the sentences below, the action verbs are underlined. Write a P over the verb if it expresses physical action; write an M over the verb if it expresses mental action.

1. Ms. Ravitz and Mr. Fischetti <u>teach</u> physical education at our school.

2. Ms. Fernandez <u>hired</u> them at the same time.

3. She <u>believes</u> they are the best for the job.

4. Ms. Ravitz <u>considered</u> a job in California.

5. They both <u>studied</u> at Springfield College.

6. Mr. Fischetti <u>said</u> the physical education program there was excellent.

7. He <u>participated</u> in many different sports.

8. Ms. Ravitz <u>remembers</u> him from her freshman English class.

9. Mr. Fischetti <u>played</u> lacrosse for Springfield; Ms. Ravitz played soccer.

10. Now Mr. Fischetti <u>coaches</u> women's lacrosse at our town's high school.

11. Ms. Ravitz <u>assists</u> the women's basketball coach.

12. Both of them <u>enjoy</u> teaching at our school.

Now use a physical action verb in a sentence of your own.

_____

Use a mental action verb in a sentence of your own.

_____

ACTION VERBS AND HELPING VERBS

Sometimes an action verb joins another verb called a **helping verb.** The helping verb comes first, and the action verb follows. The action verb is then called the **main verb.** The two verbs together are called a **verb phrase.** A verb phrase can also be a simple predicate.

Here are some sentences with verb phrases:

Our town **is celebrating** cultural diversity this month.
The kids **had run** half a mile.
The guard **will open** the museum doors.
This pilot **has flown** for many years.
The artist **was drawing** a portrait in charcoal.
I **must remember** to feed my rabbit every day.
Elise **can watch** an hour of TV after her homework is done.

These are the most common helping verbs:

am	do	have	should
are	does	is	was
can	had	may	were
could	has	must	will
did			

EXERCISE 1

Use a verb from column 1 and a helping verb from the list above to complete each sentence below.

1. cheer   Everyone _will cheer_ for the performers at the assembly.

2. move   Nadeem's family _may move_ here from Salt Lake City.

3. e-mail   Ms. Fernandez _should email_ her sister in Madrid, Spain.

4. learn   All students _could learn_ the fifty states and their capitals.

5. dance   Colette and Hope _can dance_ in the talent show.

6. skate   Kyle and Karim _must skate_ to school.

7. name   The town _should name_ the new school after Christa McAuliffe.

8. invite   Samantha _will invite_ the entire class to her party.

EXERCISE 2

Fill in the chart on the next page with the subjects, the helping verbs, and the main verbs from the following sentences.

1. Casey has watched her favorite movie many times.

2. Several students are tracing their ancestry using the Internet.

3. Arjun may go to India this summer with his grandparents.

4. Kyle is skating after school.

5. Cory must swim in the preliminary round.

6. The teachers were planning a party to introduce the new staff members.

7. Ms. Buchanan's class has studied our solar system.

8. As a young child, Elise had wanted a pony.

	SUBJECT	HELPING VERB	MAIN VERB
1.	Casey	has	watched
2.	Students	are	tracing
3.	Arjun	may	go
4.	Kyle	is	skating
5.	Cory	must	swim
6.	Teachers	were	planning
7.	class	has	studied
8.	Elise	had	wanted

THE SPECIAL VERB "BE"

When certain helping verbs are used alone, they are called *linking verbs*. Some verbs connect or link the parts of the sentence; they show a connection between the subject and the predicate.

There are five special linking verbs that are forms of the verb *to be:*

am
is
are
was
were

Here are some examples of linking verbs used in sentences:

In the early days of the U.S. space program, most astronauts **were** men.
Christa McAuliffe **is** a role model for us at our school.
She **was** a teacher who became an astronaut.
People everywhere **were** sad when she and her crewmates died.
Now both men and women **are** astronauts.
I **am** a good student in science, especially when we study space.

EXERCISE 1

In the sentences below, underline each linking verb that connects the subject to the predicate. The first one is done for you.

1. Learning long division <u>was</u> harder for me than multiplication by two digits.

2. Luis Salazar, Samantha Lonon, and Mike Dinelli are top students.

3. Social studies and science are popular subjects.

4. Keyboarding is Lisa's favorite class.

5. Computers are an important part of the school budget.

6. I am happy about the new microscopes!

7. Our teacher is a computer specialist.

8. Manipulative math was a good preparation for this year.

EXERCISE 2

Fill in the chart with the parts of the sentences below.

1. Geoff is the son of a veterinarian.

2. Casey's mom was the winner of an important science award.

3. I am the youngest in my family.

4. Andrew and Colin were lifelong friends.

5. Dr. Wisniewski is from Poland.

6. The music was loud and cheerful.

7. The restaurant is close to my house.

8. The teachers were in the faculty room before the bell.

9. I am happy I studied for the test.

10. Chanda and Megan are in the same ballet class.

1. _____   _____

2. _____   _____

3. _____   _____

4. _____   _____

5. _____   _____

6. _____   _____

7. _____   _____

8. _____   _____

9. _____   _____

10. _____   _____

When a form of the verb *to be* is used as a helping verb, the main verb will always end in *-ing.* The *-ing* verb is called the **present participle.** The two words together form the verb.

Here are some examples of *to be* used as a helping verb:

Ari's family **was saving** for a computer.

Mai Hishada's family **is leaving** for Japan at the end of the month.

Arjun and Robbie **are going** to the arcade after school.

Luis and Eduardo **were starting** a Spanish club.

I **am planning** a party for my best friend.

AGREEMENT OF SUBJECTS AND VERBS

Subjects and verbs must work together. If the subject is **singular,** the verb must also be singular. If the subject is **plural,** the verb must be plural. (*Singular* refers to one person or thing. *Plural* refers to more than one person or thing.) The verb must always match the *number* of the subject. (In grammar, *number* means singular or plural.) Whenever you have a verb and subject together, make sure both have the same number.

SINGULAR	PLURAL
I use	we use
you use	you use
he, she, it uses	they use
I play	we play
you play	you play
he, she, it plays	they play

Here are some examples of these verbs in sentences:

Adele uses her computer all the time. (subject and verb are singular)
They play chess on rainy days. (subject and verb are plural)

Here are some examples of singular subjects with singular action verbs:

I walk home from school with Tami.
Ms. Buchanan writes with her left hand.
He spells better than anyone.

Here are some examples of plural subjects with plural action verbs:

The math **charts hang** from wires high on the wall.
The soccer **players change** in the locker room.
They greet their friends every day.

EXERCISE 1

Circle the correct verb in the following sentences. (Remember: singular subjects take a singular verb; plural subjects take a plural verb.)

1. Mr. Williams (talk, talks) about the science museum.

2. We all (listen, listens) with interest.

3. He (explain, explains) the different exhibits.

4. We (like, likes) the part about the hands-on experiments.

5. The museum director (gives, give) a talk at the school.

6. She (encourage, encourages) everyone to visit.

7. Robots (collect, collects) the tickets at the door.

8. Crowds (gathers, gather) at the museum's entrance to watch them.

9. My class (get, gets) to go next Friday.

10. I (expect, expects) to have a good time.

EXERCISE 2

Circle the correct subject in the following sentences.

1. (The girl, The girls) take their time choosing a library book.

2. (He, They) organizes the materials for the teacher.

3. (The parent, The parents) park on the street next to the school.

4. (Years, Year) pass before there is another eclipse.

5. (I, She) plan to read *Number the Stars* by Lois Lowry.

6. (Tami and Hope, Tami) buy lunch at school.

VERB TENSE

Verb tense is the term used to explain how a verb shows *when* something happened. Tense or time is another way that verbs help express a sentence's meaning. Verbs can show action that is happening now (present tense), action that has already happened (past tense), and action that is going to happen (future tense).

Present tense action verbs show what is happening now.

We all **enjoy** going to the park.
Some of us **shoot** baskets or **play** other games.
Everyone **enjoys** the fresh air and sunshine.

Past tense action verbs show what happened already.

We all **enjoyed** going to the park.
Some of us **shot** baskets or **played** other games.
Everyone **enjoyed** the fresh air and sunshine.

Future tense action verbs show what will happen.

We all **will enjoy** going to the park.
Some of us **will shoot** baskets or **play** other games.
Everyone **will enjoy** the fresh air and sunshine.

EXERCISE 1

Underline the correct verb for sentences 1–5. Use the chart below to help you.

PRESENT	PAST	FUTURE
1. auditions	auditioned	will audition
2. practice	practiced	will practice
3. dance	danced	will dance
4. participates	participated	will participate
5. direct	directed	will direct

1. Students in Ms. Buchanan's class (auditioned, will audition, auditions) for the talent show tomorrow.

2. Last year almost everyone (participates, will participate, participated).

3. Professional dancers stretch and (practice, will practice, practiced) before auditions.

4. Some of the teachers (danced, will dance, dance) in the upcoming show.

5. Dr. Wisniewski always (directs, will direct, directed) the show.

Present
Present tense verbs show what is happening now. Remember that the subject and verb must agree in each sentence.

EXERCISE 1

Underline the present tense in each sentence.

1. Gym class usually (lasts, will last) about forty minutes.

2. The teachers (pick, picked) the teams when we play a game.

3. Everyone (agreed, agrees) that is the fairest way.

4. Mr. Kaplan even (will choose, chooses) the captains.

5. Ms. Buchanan (let, lets) the teammates (decide, decided).

6. Sometimes several classes (compete, competed).

7. Marcin and Andrew (will play, play) defense today.

8. Once in a while, Ms. Fernandez (refereed, referees) the game.

EXERCISE 2

Write present tense verbs for the following subjects.

1. Colette _____ the piano before she completes her homework.

2. She _____ very hard for tests.

3. Most days Colette _____ to school with Molly and Rachel.

4. Dr. King, Colette's mother, _____ them every Friday.

5. She _____ at the local hospital as a pediatrician.

6. Colette _____ to be a doctor, too.

Past

Past tense action verbs show what has already happened. To show the past tense with some verbs, you add -d, -ed, or change the y to i and add -ed. For other verbs, you show the past tense by changing the verb's form and spelling. The past tense action verbs that end in -d or -ed are called **regular past tense verbs.**

Here are some examples of regular past tense action verbs:

Yesterday in art class Josiah **painted** a picture of the tree outside his bedroom. First he **mixed** paints to get just the right colors. Then he **sketched** a rough outline of the tree and the hill behind it. Josiah **filled in** the sketch with beautiful shades of green, yellow, and brown. His teacher **praised** his colorful work. Just as he **finished,** he **spilled** paint on his shirt! Josiah **decided** to wear a smock next time.

PRESENT TENSE	+	ENDING	=	PAST TENSE
paint	+	ed	=	painted
mix	+	ed	=	mixed
sketch	+	ed	=	sketched
fill in	+	ed	=	filled in
praise	+	d	=	praised
finish	+	ed	=	finished
spill	+	ed	=	spilled
decide	+	d	=	decided

Here are two examples that show how to form the past tense of verbs that end in y:

Present tense	=	study
Change the y to *i*	=	studi
Add the ending:	+	*ed*
Past tense	=	studied

Present tense	=	carry
Change the y to *i*	=	carri
Add the ending:	+	*ed*
Past tense	=	carried

EXERCISE 1

Circle the word *present* if the verb in the sentence is in the present tense. Circle the word *past* if the verb is in the past tense.

1. present/past   The After-School Program offers a puppet-making class.

2. present/past   Ms. Pisarro teaches puppet-making and script writing.

3. present/past   The program also provides a homework club.

4. present/past   The high school soccer coach conducted a soccer clinic.

5. present/past   Even Ms. Fernandez, the principal, participates in the program.

6. present/past   She does a class in telling and writing jokes.

7. present/past   The students loved Adam's chicken jokes.

8. present/past   Nadeem Jordan's father offers a self-defense course.

9. present/past   Many students enroll in that class.

10. present/past   The baby-sitting class provided a mini first-aid course.

11. present/past   The school nurse trained the students in first aid.

12. present/past   Mrs. Wisniewski teaches hip-hop.

EXERCISE 2

Underline each regular past tense verb.

1. The Parent/Teacher Association raised money for special assemblies.

2. They sponsored a book fair, a used-equipment sale, and an auction.

3. The parents and teachers reached their goal of $10,000.

4. The principal formed a committee of parents, teachers, and students.

5. This committee selected the assemblies and arranged the calendar.

6. At one assembly actors performed with gestures and no words.

7. These actors presented a play about respect and good manners.

8. The actors called their performance "mime."

9. Others assemblies featured scientists.

10. One scientist experimented with baking soda and vinegar to create a chemical reaction.

11. Another scientist presented a show about motion.

12. A famous children's author and his illustrator also appeared.

13. The illustrator sketched so fast the students called her "The Wizard."

14. She explained how she worked with authors to create the story's characters.

15. The illustrator picked three students from the audience to assist her.

16. The author created stories and characters for all ages.

17. His presentation helped students understand how a book is written.

18. Students throughout the grades appreciated all of the assemblies.

EXERCISE 3

Change the present tense verbs below to the past tense. Write the past tense form on the line after each verb.

PRESENT   PAST

1. ask   _____

2. try   _____

3. use   _____

4. worry   _____

5. believe   _____

6. spy   _____

7. talk   _____

EXERCISE 4

Write four sentences about the things you do in your spare time. Use present tense verbs in two of the sentences and past tense verbs in two of them.

1. _____

2. _____

3. _____

4. _____

Future

Future tense action verbs show what will happen in time to come. Verbs in the future tense have the word *will* before the main verb. The two verbs together form a verb phrase.

Here are some examples of future tense action verb phrases:

Several classes **will go** to the library next Tuesday. Mr. Dunn, the librarian, **will instruct** each class in research skills. He **will show** the students how to use the online catalog to look for books. Also, Mr. Dunn **will coordinate** students' research with the reading program that the teachers **will follow** this year.

Here are the verb phrases from those sentences:

will go
will instruct
will show
will coordinate
will follow

These are the main verbs:

go
instruct
show
coordinate
follow

EXERCISE 1

Underline the future tense verb phrases in the following sentences.

1. The students will choose which authors to study.

2. A group of five students will read Roald Dahl's books.

3. Mike Dinelli will join the group reading Gary Paulsen's books.

4. Nadeem, Sara, and Daniel will choose works by Katherine Paterson.

5. Mr. Dunn will gather biographical information about the authors.

6. The Internet will help him get current data.

7. The library will buzz with activity.

8. The groups will illustrate their reports.

EXERCISE 2

Write three sentences that tell what you will do when you go home today. Use a future tense verb phrase in each. An example is done for you.

I will call Grandma as soon as I get home. I will tell her about my A on the spelling test. She will tell me that she is proud.

_____

_____

_____

_____

_____

_____

LOOKING AGAIN AT PRESENT, PAST, FUTURE

EXERCISE 1

Read the sentences below and place the underlined verbs or verb phrases in the correct column.

1. Several classes <u>are studying</u> families.

2. In their journals, they <u>wrote</u> about what they <u>think</u> makes a family.

3. Alanna <u>said</u> that her mother's best friend <u>is</u> like a second mother.

4. Many students <u>want</u> to honor people they care about.

5. The students in one class <u>will create</u> a quilt.

6. Everyone <u>will design</u> a section of the quilt.

7. They <u>will make</u> the quilt bright and colorful.

8. A group of parents <u>will help</u> with the stitching.

9. Ms. Fernandez <u>belongs</u> to a quilting club.

10. She <u>will decorate</u> the border with the names of family members.

11. Everyone <u>discussed</u> the people they love.

PRESENT   PAST   FUTURE

_____   _____   _____

_____   _____   _____

_____   _____   _____

_____   _____

                                             _____

EXERCISE 2

On the lines below, write a paragraph about a person who is important to you. Be sure to tell who the person is, what this person is like, and what he or she means to you.

_____

_____

_____

_____

_____

_____

VERB FORMS

Past Tense Regular Verb Forms

There are **regular** and **irregular** past tense forms of action verbs. Regular verbs add a *-d* or an *-ed* to show the past tense. (You have already learned some of these verbs.) *Regular* means they follow a set pattern. Here are four ways to make regular verbs show past tense:

1. add *-ed* to most verbs
   print   printed
   look   looked

2. add *-d* when the verb ends with e
   decide   decided
   race   raced

3. double the consonant and add *-ed* when the verb ends in a single consonant after a short vowel
   pat   patted
   drop   dropped
   tip   tipped

4. change the *y* to *i* and add *-ed* when the verb ends in a *y* after a consonant
   try   tried
   fry   fried
   deny   denied

Study the patterns of these regular past tense action verbs.

EXERCISE 1

Change the verb in column 1 to the past form and write it in the sentence.

1. hope   The kids _____ the forecast for snow was correct.

2. watch   They _____ the Weather Channel all evening.

3. snow   During the night it _____ heavily.

4. hop   Robbie _____ out of bed to look outside.

5. call   He _____ to his mother to ask if there was school.

6. reply   "Not today!" she _____.

7. hurry   Robbie _____ to phone his best friend.

8. plan   Together they _____ their day off.

Past Tense Irregular Verb Forms

Some verbs do not follow a regular pattern. Instead of adding *-d* or *-ed* to show past tense, they change their spelling and become a different word. They are called **irregular verbs.** Because they do not follow a pattern, you must memorize them. The most common ones are printed in the chart below.

Notice that the verbs in the third column all have a helping verb. This is a different type of past tense; it is called the **past participle.** A participle is a word formed from a verb. When it is used with a helping verb, as it is here, it is the main part of verb.

PRESENT	PAST	PAST PARTICIPLE
begin	began	(have, has, had) begun
break	broke	(have, has, had) broken
bring	brought	(have, has, had) brought
come	came	(have, has, had) come
do	did	(have, has, had) done
drive	drove	(have, has, had) driven
eat	ate	(have, has, had) eaten
give	gave	(have, has, had) given
go	went	(have, has, had) gone
grow	grew	(have, has, had) grown
know	knew	(have, has, had) known
make	made	(have, has, had) made
run	ran	(have, has, had) run
say	said	(have, has, had) said
see	saw	(have, has, had) seen
sing	sang	(have, has, had) sung
speak	spoke	(have, has, had) spoken
take	took	(have, has, had) taken
tell	told	(have, has, had) told
throw	threw	(have, has, had) thrown
wear	wore	(have, has, had) worn
write	wrote	(have, has, had) written

Read the sentences below. Notice how the irregular verbs are used.

Cory Cheng's father **drove** Ramon, Noel, and Sam to basketball practice.
They **brought** their own practice balls.
Everyone **wore** a practice jersey.

Coach Greenberg **took** attendance before they began.
The coach **had given** them the rules of the game to learn.
Some players **knew** the rules already.

EXERCISE 1

Write about something that happened to you that made you laugh out loud or made you feel another strong emotion. Write in the past tense and use at least five to seven sentences. Writing about a meaningful moment in one's own life is called *memoir writing*. In the box below your story, draw a picture of yourself as you feel the emotion you wrote about.

EXERCISE 2

Fill in the correct form of the verb to show past action.

1. know   Rachel _____ her parents were planning a surprise party.

2. bring   Eduardo had _____ his grandfather to school.

3. take   It _____ the class a long time to learn the difficult song.

4. break   Casey had _____ the school record for the mile run.

5. eat   Ms. Fernandez _____ lunch with the teachers.

6. do   The students _____ line dancing in physical education class.

7. grow   Ben has _____ four inches in the last nine months.

8. go   Grahame _____ with his aunt and uncle to the bus station.

MAIN PARTS OF REGULAR VERBS

The chart below shows the four main parts of some regular action verbs.

PRESENT	PRESENT PARTICIPLE (-ing form)	PAST*	PAST PARTICIPLE (uses helping verbs have, has, had)
appear	appearing	appeared	(have, has, had) appeared
believe	believing	believed	(have, has, had) believed
borrow	borrowing	borrowed	(have, has, had) borrowed
carry	carrying	carried	(have, has, had) carried
climb	climbing	climbed	(have, has, had) climbed
close	closing	closed	(have, has, had) closed
direct	directing	directed	(have, has, had) directed
explore	exploring	explored	(have, has, had) explored
help	helping	helped	(have, has, had) helped
hop	hopping	hopped	(have, has, had) hopped
learn	learning	learned	(have, has, had) learned
multiply	multiplying	multiplied	(have, has, had) multiplied
occur	occurring	occurred	(have, has, had) occurred
plan	planning	planned	(have, has, had) planned

PRESENT	PRESENT PARTICIPLE (-ing form)	PAST*	PAST PARTICIPLE (uses helping verbs have, has, had)
receive	receiving	received	(have, has, had) received
train	training	trained	(have, has, had) trained
wonder	wondering	wondered	(have, has, had) wondered
work	working	worked	(have, has, had) worked

*Be sure to notice that in regular verbs the past and the past participle forms are exactly alike. The only difference between the forms of the past and the past participle is that the past participle must have a helping verb.

The first column shows the present tense.

Example: I talk about being an astronaut.

The second column shows the present participle or *-ing* form.

Example: I am talking about being an astronaut.

The third column shows the past tense.

Example: I talked about being an astronaut.

The fourth column shows the past participle. The past participle always uses a helping verb.

Example: I had talked about being an astronaut.

REMEMBER: These are the patterns of regular past tense action verbs:
1. add *-ed* to most verbs
   print – printed   look – looked
2. add *-d* when the verb ends with *e*
   decide – decided   race – raced
3. double the consonant and add *-ed* when the verb ends in a single consonant after a short vowel
   pat – patted   drop – dropped   tip – tipped
4. change the *y* to *i* and add *-ed* when the verb ends in a *y* after a consonant
   try – tried   fry – fried   deny – denied

EXERCISE 1

Underline the correct verb form in each sentence.

1. Ms. Buchanan's math class (has learned, learning) about money.

2. They (have charted, charting) examples from their math book.

3. Samantha is (wondered, wondering) if they could sell real items.

4. The rest of the class was (planning, plan).

5. Ms. Buchanan said she and Ms. Fernandez were (explore, exploring) the idea.

6. Several students (talked, talking) about money for recess equipment.

7. Others (started, starting) a discussion about games for younger students.

8. Everyone (deciding, decided) a bake sale would raise money.

9. Many volunteers (baked, baking) cupcakes and cookies.

10. Students (decorating, decorated) posters for advertising.

11. Ms. Buchanan's students took turns (counting, counted) and (checking, checked) the money.

EXERCISE 2

Use the form of the verb given in parentheses to complete the following sentences.

1. (present participle of *plan*)

   The Hishada family is _____ a trip to Santa Fe, New Mexico.

2. (present of *wish*)

   I _____ I could go with them.

3. (past of *receive*)

   They _____ information from their travel agent.

4. (past participle of *explore*)

   Mai has _____ the Internet for interesting places to visit.

5. (past of *learn*)

The family _____ some conversational Spanish.

6. (present participle of *practice*)

They are _____ a little each night.

MAIN PARTS OF IRREGULAR VERBS

The chart below shows the four main parts of some irregular action verbs.

REMEMBER: Irregular verbs change their spelling instead of adding *-ed* or *-d* to show past tense. You should begin to memorize these verb forms.

The first column shows the present tense.

Example: I go to the beach every summer.

The second column shows the present participle or *-ing* form.

Example: I am going to the beach this summer.

The third column shows the past tense.

Example: I went to the beach last summer.

The fourth column shows the past participle. The past participle always uses a helping verb.

Example: I have gone to the beach every summer for three years.

PRESENT	PRESENT PARTICIPLE	PAST	PAST PARTICIPLE
begin	beginning	began	(has, have, had) begun
break	breaking	broke	(has, have, had) broken
bring	bringing	brought	(has, have, had) brought
choose	choosing	chose	(has, have, had) chosen
come	coming	came	(has, have, had) come

PRESENT	PRESENT PARTICIPLE	PAST	PAST PARTICIPLE
do	doing	did	(has, have, had) done
drive	driving	drove	(has, have, had) driven
eat	eating	ate	(has, have, had) eaten
forget	forgetting	forgot	(has, have, had) forgotten
give	giving	gave	(has, have, had) given
go	going	went	(has, have, had) gone
grow	growing	grew	(has, have, had) grown
keep	keeping	kept	(has, have, had) kept
know	knowing	knew	(has, have, had) known
make	making	made	(has, have, had) made
ring	ringing	rang	(has, have, had) rung
run	running	ran	(has, have, had) run
say	saying	said	(has, have, had) said
see	seeing	saw	(has, have, had) seen
sing	singing	sang	(has, have, had) sung
speak	speaking	spoke	(has, have, had) spoken
take	taking	took	(has, have, had) taken
tell	telling	told	(has, have, had) told
throw	throwing	threw	(has, have, had) thrown
wear	wearing	wore	(has, have, had) worn
write	writing	wrote	(has, have, had) written

In the next exercise, you will read two poems. One is a Japanese form called a haiku. Though there are different kinds of haiku, the poem here has three lines with five syllables in the first line, seven in the second line, and five in the last line. The second poem is called a diamonte poem, because its shape looks like a diamond. There are two words in the first line, four in the second line, six in the third line, eight in the fourth line, six in the fifth line, four in the sixth line, and two in the last line.

EXERCISE 1

In each of the poems below, circle only the irregular verbs.

HAIKU

Branches broke, birds spoke,
Carrying sounds of Nature.
Listen to her call.

DIAMONTE

I wore
Knee pads, a helmet,
All the stuff of the sport.
Now I must make the run. Whoooosh! Whoa!
Can't break speed! Must keep pace!
Will not give up!
Come down.

EXERCISE 2

Look at the chart on pages 56–57 and choose eight irregular verbs that you plan to memorize first. Write the four main parts of each of the verbs that you choose.

PRESENT	PRESENT PARTICIPLE (-ing form)	PAST	PAST PARTICIPLE (uses helping verbs have, has, had)
1. _____	_____	_____	_____
2. _____	_____	_____	_____
3. _____	_____	_____	_____
4. _____	_____	_____	_____
5. _____	_____	_____	_____
6. _____	_____	_____	_____
7. _____	_____	_____	_____
8. _____	_____	_____	_____

EXERCISE 3

Now choose four of the eight verbs from your chart in Exercise 2. Use each in a sentence and then write which form of the verb you used. An example is done for you.

SENTENCE   VERB FORM

1. Lori has chosen a puppy for a pet. _____   past participle

2. _____   _____

3. _____   _____

4. _____   _____

5. _____   _____

ACTION VERBS WITH "NOT"

Sometimes writers and speakers want to say what did not happen—as you can see from this sentence, the word *not* describes what is being done. It is called a **negative,** because it describes something that does not occur. *Not* follows the helping verb in the verb phrase. Look at some other examples:

> Luis **is not** swimming at the meet on Saturday.
> Colette **could not** go to the movies.
> Ameesh **has not** found his sneakers.
> Hope and Megan **did not** buy the tickets.
> Ted **had not** practiced with the team.

Contractions with *Not*

A **contraction** is a word that is made up of two words with at least one letter taken out (deleted). An apostrophe (') replaces the deleted letter or letters. When writers and speakers want to say what did not happen, they often use a contraction, such as *doesn't* (which stands for *does not*), *isn't* (*is not*), or *didn't* (*did not*). To write this contraction, combine the helping verb and the word *not*. Delete the *o* in *not* and replace it with an apostrophe: *n't*. Then add *-n't* to the end of the helping verb.

Look at the examples:

> Luis **isn't** swimming at the meet on Saturday.
> Colette **couldn't** go to the movies.
> Ameesh **hasn't** found his sneakers.
> Hope and Megan **didn't** buy the tickets.
> Ted **hadn't** practiced with the team.

In the following contractions *not* becomes *n't* and is added to the end of the helping verb. The exceptions are *will not* and *cannot*. The spelling of the verb *will* changes when it is combined with *not* to form the contraction *won't.* (Notice that *won't* is easier to say than *willn't*.) The contraction *can't* is a shortened form of the word *cannot*. Both the second *n* and the *o* are deleted.

are not	aren't
cannot	can't
could not	couldn't
did not	didn't
does not	doesn't
do not	don't
had not	hadn't
has not	hasn't
have not	haven't
is not	isn't
should not	shouldn't
was not	wasn't
were not	weren't
will not	won't
would not	wouldn't

EXERCISE 1

Write the contraction for each word or pair of words below. The first one is done for you.

1. did not   didn't

2. could not   _____

3. is not   _____

4. will not   _____

5. has not   _____

6. do not   _____

7. was not   _____

8. cannot   _____

9. have not   _____

10. were not   _____

EXERCISE 2

In the sentences below, a word or words are underlined. Write the contraction for these words on the line in front of each sentence.

1. _____ Mr. Fischetti, the physical education teacher, <u>cannot</u> have the scavenger hunt until next week.

2. _____ The ground <u>was not</u> dry enough from the recent storm.

3. _____ He <u>had not</u> wanted anyone to get wet searching for the hidden objects.

4. _____ The students <u>could not</u> wait because it was one of their favorite activities.

5. _____ They <u>did not</u> waste any time getting started on Monday.

6. _____ The parents could watch, but they <u>were not</u> allowed to give clues.

7. _____ Mr. Kaplan's class <u>has not</u> won in seven years.

8. _____ Winners <u>do not</u> act impulsively; they read the clues carefully.

EXERCISE 3

On the line in front of each sentence, write the word or words that make up the underlined contraction.

1. _____ Kelly isn't going to soccer practice.

2. _____ John and Geoff haven't eaten lunch yet.

3. _____ Kyle shouldn't play kickball with his sprained ankle.

4. _____ Alyson and Jill aren't sure if they should study together.

5. _____ Noel doesn't have a color printer.

6. _____ Mr. Williams won't give homework the night of the skating party.

7. _____ Marcin wouldn't forget to bring his lacrosse stick to school.

8. _____ The teachers hadn't known about the fire drill.

WRITING WITH VERBS IN THE SAME TENSE

All writers should spend time making their writing clear for the reader. One important way to do this is to keep all verbs in the same tense. (Remember that the tense of a verb tells you whether the action is past, present, or future.)

Present tense action verbs show what is happening now.
Past tense action verbs show what happened already.
Future tense action verbs show what will happen.

A writer should ask, "Is the tense of my verbs consistent?" *Consistent* means unchanging.

EXERCISE 1

Look at the paragraph below. All of the verbs except two are in the present tense; two verbs are in the past tense. This may confuse the reader about when the action is taking place.

Matt teaches Attean how to read the English language. In return, Attean teaches Matt how to read the signs of nature in the forest. Although Matt respected Attean and his abilities, Attean mocked Matt's clumsiness.
(Based on the story *The Sign of the Beaver* by Elizabeth George Speare)

Rewrite the paragraph on the lines below, making the verb tense consistent. Put all of the verbs in the present tense.

_____

_____

_____

_____

_____

_____

_____

EXERCISE 2

Correctly rewrite the paragraph below by putting all verbs in the present tense.

Both children and adults love the Harry Potter books. Harry's adventures captured the imagination because the books are filled with fantastic tales of wizardry. These spellbinding stories leave the reader craving more. Most of all, the Harry Potter books were fun!

_____

_____

_____

_____

_____

EXERCISE 3

The paragraph below discusses events that happened in the past. Rewrite the paragraph so that all verbs are in the past tense.

Yesterday I went to a fair at my brother's school. The magician at the fair was very entertaining. First he takes a deck of cards and asks me to pick one. Then he shuffled all the cards and fanned them out. My card is on top! Somehow he knows which card I picked.

_____

_____

_____

_____

_____

DIAGRAMMING SIMPLE SUBJECTS AND SIMPLE PREDICATES WITH A VERB PHRASE

This section shows how to diagram simple subjects and simple predicates when the simple predicate is a verb phrase. A verb phrase is made up of two or more verbs, the main verb and the helping verbs.

The simple subject and simple predicate are written on a horizontal line (_____). They are separated from each other by a vertical or up-and-down line (|) that intersects or cuts through the horizontal line.

Look at the sentence below.

Mother is laughing.

The simple subject is *Mother*. The simple predicate is the verb phrase *is laughing*. They are diagrammed as follows:

Mother | is laughing

Remember that there is no punctuation in the diagram.
Look at the next sentence.

I should have called you earlier.

The simple subject is *I*. The simple predicate is the verb phrase *should have called*. They are diagrammed as follows:

I | should have called

Place the simple subjects and simple predicates from the sentences below in the graphic organizers provided. The first one is done for you.

1. The audience was laughing.

2. The actors were studying their lines.

3. The basketball team had practiced after school.

4. Tyler should have written a note of apology.

5. Anything can happen in a tie game.

EXERCISE 2

In the following sentences, draw the graphic organizers yourself. Write the simple subject before the vertical line. Write the simple predicate or verb phrase after the vertical line. Use a ruler to help you make straight lines.

1. Everyone is talking about the new science fiction movie.

2. Noel's trombone was left in the music room.

3. I will vote for the best candidate.

4. The rain has been falling for five hours.

5. Meteor showers will appear suddenly in the night sky.

VERB REVIEW EXERCISES

REMEMBER: Action verbs show or tell what the action is. Linking verbs connect the subject and the predicate. The most common linking verbs are *am*, *is*, *are*, *was*, and *were*.

EXERCISE 1

Find the action verb in each sentence and circle it. The subject is underlined in each sentence.

1. <u>Dr. Wisniewski</u> talked to the students about instrumental music.

2. In the past, only <u>sixth graders</u> had played instruments.

3. This year the <u>school board</u> allowed fourth and fifth grade students to play.

4. <u>Dr. Wisniewski</u> needed an assistant.

5. <u>Kira Larsson</u> applied for the music assistantship at Christa McAuliffe School.

6. <u>She</u> had studied music in Boston.

7. The <u>board</u> hired Ms. Larsson as Dr. Wisniewski's assistant.

8. <u>Ms. Fernandez</u> introduced her to the teachers and students.

9. <u>Ms. Larsson</u> explained the various instruments to the new players.

10. Many <u>students</u> enrolled in the recorder class.

EXERCISE 2

Circle the verb or verb phrase in each sentence. Then, on the line next to the sentence, tell which form of the verb is used: present, present participle, past, or past participle.

1. Our class is planning student presentations. _____

2. We must talk for fifteen minutes on a topic of our choice. _____

3. I thought of many ideas. _____

4. Maybe I could do a report on my favorite animals, turtles. _____

5. Kavita is interviewing her grandfather. _____

6. He has had many adventures in his life. _____

7. Daniel's topic sounds fascinating. _____

8. His report discusses his visit to circus camp. _____

9. Students' families are invited to the presentations. _____

10. We are all excited about the big day. _____

EXERCISE 3

Complete the chart below by adding the missing verb forms.

PRESENT	PRESENT PARTICIPLE	PAST	PAST PARTICIPLE
1. borrow	_____	borrowed	(has, have, had) borrowed
2. _____	bringing	brought	(has, have, had) brought
3. climb	climbing	_____	(has, have, had) climbed
4. do	doing	did	(has, have, had) _____
5. _____	driving	_____	(has, have, had) driven
6. explore	_____	explored	(has, have, had) explored
7. fall	falling	fell	(has, have, had) _____
8. give	giving	gave	(has, have, had) _____
9. help	_____	helped	(has, have, had) helped
10. join	joining	_____	(has, have, had) joined
11. _____	knowing	knew	(has, have, had) known
12. learn	_____	learned	(has, have, had) learned

PRESENT	PRESENT PARTICIPLE	PAST	PAST PARTICIPLE
13. make	making	_____	(has, have, had) made
14. occur	occurring	occurred	(has, have, had) _____
15. run	running	_____	(has, have, had) run
16. skip	_____	skipped	(has, have, had) skipped
17. _____	singing	sang	(has, have, had) sung
18. _____	taking	took	(has, have, had) taken
19. wonder	_____	wondered	(has, have, had) wondered
20. wear	wearing	_____	(has, have, had) worn

EXERCISE 4

Underline only the action verbs in the following sentences. Circle the linking verbs.

1. Many students are aware of trash around our school.
2. Careless people drop trash on the ground.
3. It is annoying, especially on a windy day.
4. We are trying to solve this problem.
5. Our student government formed a committee.
6. There were fifteen volunteers.
7. Several members offered boxes of trash bags.
8. "Clean up Christa's School" became our motto.
9. Three days a week, we patrol the school yard for trash.
10. Sometimes more people join and help.

EXERCISE 5

Choose the correct linking verb to complete each sentence.

am

is

are

was

were

1. Nutrition _____ an important topic today.

2. There _____ foods crucial to our health.

3. Years ago there _____ not as much information.

4. Many people _____ unaware of the necessary vitamins and minerals in food.

5. I _____ careful to eat enough fruit and vegetables.

REMEMBER: A verb phrase is made up of a helping verb and a main verb. These are some of the most common helping verbs:

am	does	must
are	had	should
can	has	was
could	have	were
did	is	will
do	may	

EXERCISE 6

Each sentence below has a verb phrase. Circle the helping verbs and underline the main verbs.

1. Some students can choose how they travel to school.

2. One day they may ride a bike.

3. The law states they must wear helmets.

4. Many will walk on a fine day.

5. Others may live too far away.

6. They could ride the bus.

7. Some parents will drop their children off on their way to work.

8. Sometimes students have come in late.

9. They should bring an excuse.

10. A teacher does understand a good reason.

REMEMBER: Verbs and subjects must agree in number. Use the singular form of a verb with a singular subject; use a plural verb with a plural subject.

EXERCISE 7

Circle the correct subject or verb in the sentences below.

1. Each generation (study, studies) the multiplication tables.

2. (Student, Students) learn the facts carefully.

3. This year Ms. Buchanan (teach, teaches) facts to the beat of rap music.

4. The (child, children) love it!

5. Some classes (have, has) contests to see who is the fastest at flash cards.

6. Division facts (follows, follow) multiplication facts.

7. Mr. Williams' class (plays, play) math games.

8. (Parent, Parents) remember their own math drills.

9. Students (challenges, challenge) each other in speed drills.

10. Christa McAuliffe School (participates, participate) in the National Math Olympiad.

REMEMBER: Present tense verbs show what is happening now. Past tense verbs show what happened already. Future tense verbs show what will happen.

EXERCISE 8

Read the following sentences. In column 1, write the verbs in each sentence. In column 2, label each verb *present, past,* or *future.*

1. Pets come in many varieties.

2. Some families have decided on the more common pets.

3. Puppies will bring joy to a large number of people.

4. Guinea pigs squeak and scratch.

5. Ferret owners formed a club.

6. Cats will remain a favorite.

7. Hamsters stuff their mouths with food.

8. The slithering snakes in the pet store delighted Elise.

9. Grahame's parents will buy him a gerbil.

10. A pet fair takes place at our school every spring.

VERB   VERB TENSE

1. _____   _____

2. _____   _____

3. _____   _____

4. _____   _____

5. _____   _____

6. _____   _____

7. _____   _____

VERB	VERB TENSE
8. _____	_____
9. _____	_____
10. _____	_____

REMEMBER: Regular verbs add a *-d* or *-ed* to show the past tense. When the verb ends in a single consonant that is after a short vowel, double the consonant and add *-ed*. Change the *y* to *i* and add *-ed* when the verb ends in a *y* that follows a consonant.

EXERCISE 9

In the chart below, the present and the present participle are given to you. Fill in the past form of each.

PRESENT	PRESENT PARTICIPLE	PAST
worry	worrying	_____
explain	explaining	_____
skip	skipping	_____
collect	collecting	_____
organize	organizing	_____
carry	carrying	_____
cry	crying	_____
serve	serving	_____
surf	surfing	_____
excite	exciting	_____
plan	planning	_____
clap	clapping	_____

REMEMBER: Some verbs do not follow a regular pattern. They are called irregular verbs.

EXERCISE 10

Rewrite each sentence, using the correct past form of the irregular verb.

1. The girls (sing) jingles as they jumped rope.

_____

2. The skaters (go) past the duck pond.

_____

3. Tyler (break) his bat when he popped the fly.

_____

4. Colette (run) and (throw) the ball.

_____

5. The catcher (wear) a mitt.

_____

6. The third baseman (drive) the ball to home plate.

_____

7. The boys and girls (bring) their lacrosse sticks to the park.

_____

8. Casey's friends (come) to play hopscotch.

_____

9. As the players (grow), basketball became easier.

_____

10. Eduardo (begin) swimming lessons.

_____

REMEMBER: Regular action verbs have four main parts. They are **present, present participle** (-*ing* form), **past,** and **past participle** (uses helping verbs). In regular verbs the forms of the past and the past participle are exactly alike.

EXERCISE 11

Fill in the missing verbs in the chart below.

PRESENT	PRESENT PARTICIPLE	PAST	PAST PARTICIPLE
create	_____	created	(has, have, had) created
_____	directing	directed	(has, have, had) directed
explore	exploring	_____	(has, have, had) explored
clip	_____	clipped	(has, have, had) _____
_____	marrying	married	(has, have, had) married
zoom	_____	zoomed	(has, have, had) zoomed
appear	appearing	_____	(has, have, had) appeared
sprinkle	sprinkling	sprinkled	(has, have, had) _____
_____	hopping	hopped	(has, have, had) hopped
zap	_____	zapped	(has, have, had) zapped
print	printing	_____	(has, have, had) printed
smile	smiling	_____	(has, have, had) smiled
_____	preferring	preferred	(has, have, had) _____
imagine	_____	_____	(has, have, had) imagined
_____	pretending	pretended	(has, have, had) _____

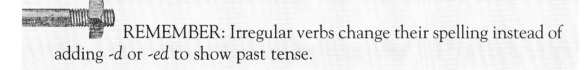

REMEMBER: Irregular verbs change their spelling instead of adding -*d* or -*ed* to show past tense.

EXERCISE 12

Circle the correct past tense form of the verb in each sentence below.

1. Ben Ward's dad (had wrote, wrote) a sports column for a major newspaper.

2. Mr. Ward (had known, know) an amazing number of professional sports figures.

3. He (has spoken, speak) to athletes, coaches, and trainers.

4. His column (kept, keeps) people interested.

5. He often (gave, given) his opinion with a touch of humor.

6. Mr. Ward (taken, took) a first-place award in a national contest for sports writers.

7. His words (drew, drawing) a mental picture of an athlete's dream of success.

8. Mr. Ward (does, did) a writer's workshop for Ben's class.

9. Ben (told, tell) his dad that he wanted to play professional ball.

10. He (says, said) he (chooses, has chosen) to focus on soccer.

 REMEMBER: When combining verbs with the word *not*, replace the *o* in *not* with an apostrophe and add *-n't* to the end of the helping verb.

EXERCISE 13

Rewrite each sentence, using a contraction in place of the underlined words.

1. The basketball team <u>did not</u> practice on Monday.

_____

2. We <u>could not</u> go on the picnic because of the rain.

_____

3. A few of the girls <u>were not</u> dancing in the recital.

_____

4. The principal <u>does not</u> forget anyone's name.

_____

5. Tyler <u>has not</u> answered my e-mail.

_____

 REMEMBER: To make your meaning clear to the reader, keep all verbs in the same tense.

EXERCISE 14

A book review is written in the present tense. Choose a favorite book and use the lines below to write a review. Give a brief plot summary, and then explore the setting and characters.

_____

_____

_____

_____

_____

_____

_____

_____

_____

_____

_____

_____

REMEMBER: A diagram is an organized picture of the words in a sentence that shows what the words do. It begins with two lines, the horizontal line (_____) and the vertical line (|) that intersects it.

EXERCISE 15

Place the simple subjects and the simple predicates in the diagrams provided.

1. The teachers have prepared for the new science program.

2. The boy in the blue and yellow baseball cap is a new student.

3. Professional athletes practice many hours each day.

4. Horror movies can be very scary.

5. An astronaut's training includes simulations of life in outer space.

RIDGEWOOD GRAMMAR

Draw diagrams for the sentences below. Place the simple subjects in front of the vertical line; place the simple predicates after the vertical line.

1. The Harry Potter series can be bought at any bookstore.

2. *Charlotte's Web* remains a favorite of young and old.

3. The Cinderella story has many versions.

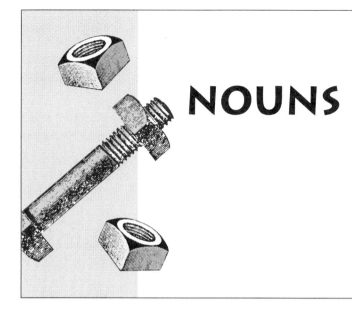

NOUNS

ABOUT NOUNS

Far above my **head**
A merry **chirping** carries
Over the **rustling** of the **leaves**
And the **whispering** of the **wind.**
The **voice** of a **robin,**
A **mother**, loving her **children,**
Sings of **joy** and **hope** and **pride**
From her **nest** perched high on a **branch.**
Regal, stately, earthy, bold,
Bringing **pleasure** to the **nest,**
Pleasure and **trust** and **life**
Far above my **head**.

This poem uses many **nouns.** A noun is a word that is used to name people, places, objects/things, ideas, and feelings. Now listen and read along in your book while your teacher reads the poem a second time. Notice the words that are underlined; they are all nouns.

In a sentence nouns can do several things:
Nouns can tell **who** is doing something.

Example: The **robin** sang.

Who sang? The robin.

Nouns can name the **place.**

Example: The nest was on a **branch.**

Where was the nest? On a branch.

Nouns can answer the question, **"What?"**

Example: The **chirping** carried.

What carried? The chirping.

Nouns can name an **idea.**

Example: The song expressed **trust.**

What idea did the song express? Trust.

Nouns can name a **feeling.**

Example: The mother sang of **joy.**

What feeling did the mother have? Joy.

Here are some other examples of nouns:

PEOPLE	PLACES	OBJECTS/ THINGS	IDEAS	FEELINGS
doctor	field	computer	responsibility	joy
father	theater	chair	cooperation	love
minister	classroom	hat	flexibility	pleasure
cousin	elevator	instrument	courage	excitement
grandmother	library	chart	intelligence	sadness

EXERCISE 1

Write a poem of your own (about six lines long) on the lines below. You may choose to have your poem rhyme or not. Your poem may be about anything in nature, such as birds, a season, trees, or animals.

Title:_____

_____

_____

_____

_____

_____

_____

Make a list below of words you used that name people, places, objects/things, ideas, or feelings.

_____

_____

_____

_____

_____

_____

_____

_____

_____

_____

_____

EXERCISE 2

Underline the nouns in the sentences below.

NOUNS THAT NAME PEOPLE

1. The ancient Egyptians were the first people to measure a year with exactness.

2. Men and women knew the best time to plant crops was after the Nile River overflowed each year.

3. Egyptian priests noticed that between each overflowing the moon rose twelve times.

NOUNS THAT NAME PLACES

1. In Egypt, a certain bright star would rise just before the sun rose.

2. People around the world wanted a calendar.

3. Julius Caesar, the leader of Rome, ordered that every year have 365 and 1/4 days.

NOUNS THAT NAME OBJECTS/THINGS

1. A calendar based on the moon is called a lunar calendar.

2. A solar calendar relies on the number of days it takes the earth to go around the sun.

3. This type of calendar has an extra quarter of a day each year.

NOUNS THAT NAME IDEAS

1. There was confusion about the extra quarter of a day.

2. Consistency was needed.

3. Creativity helped solve the problem.

1. Inserting a leap year every fourth year led to satisfaction with the calendar.

2. Julius Caesar must have felt pride in straightening out the problem.

3. He might have felt disappointment if he had learned that in 1582 Pope Gregory XIII had to change the calendar again to help ensure accuracy.

EXERCISE 3

Name three people you know and the feelings you have for each of them. For example: love, admiration, loyalty, pride.

NAMES   FEELINGS

1. _____   1. _____

2. _____   2. _____

3. _____   3. _____

Name three places you like to go and the objects/things you see there.

PLACES   OBJECTS/THINGS

1. _____   1. _____

2. _____   2. _____

3. _____   3. _____

On the lines below, write three sentences about one of the people you named above.

_____

_____

_____

_____

_____

Write the underlined nouns in the following paragraphs under the correct headings on the chart below. Write each noun only once. You do not need to write on every line.

<u>Caves</u> are linked with the <u>history</u> of <u>humans</u>. In the Stone Age, caves were the winter <u>dwellings</u> for <u>people</u> who had no other <u>shelter</u>. They are deep, hollow <u>places</u> in the rocky <u>sides</u> of <u>hills</u> or <u>cliffs</u>.

Ancient people had different <u>beliefs</u> about caves. In <u>Greece</u>, many people believed caves were <u>temples</u> of some of their gods, such as <u>Zeus</u>, <u>Pan</u>, <u>Dionysus</u>, and <u>Hades</u>. In Greece and <u>Rome</u>, some <u>believers</u> thought caves were the <u>home</u> of mythical <u>maidens</u> who predicted the future. As Rome's <u>power</u> grew, <u>followers</u> of other religions came to the <u>city</u>. Despite the <u>diversity</u> of their beliefs most people worshipped together in <u>peace</u>, taking <u>pride</u> in their heritage.

<u>Interest</u> in caves is common today, because many people still seek <u>knowledge</u> about these beautiful natural features.

PEOPLE	PLACES	OBJECTS/ THINGS	IDEAS	FEELINGS
_____	_____	_____	_____	_____
_____	_____	_____	_____	_____
_____	_____	_____	_____	_____
_____	_____	_____	_____	_____
_____	_____	_____	_____	_____
_____	_____	_____	_____	
_____	_____	_____	_____	
_____	_____	_____		
_____	_____			
_____				
_____				

COMMON NOUNS

A **common noun** is a name for any one of a whole class of persons, places, objects/things, ideas, or feelings. It may be the name of a single thing or a group of things. Common nouns begin with lowercase letters.

Here are some examples of common nouns:

plant	noises	sleepiness
animals	city	ballpark
time	pilot	nurse
book	understanding	station

All of the nouns in the list on page 81 are common nouns.

EXERCISE 1

Underline the common nouns in the following sentences.

1. Some people took longer to get to school today.

2. Karim's bus traveled slowly because of the fog.

3. Some students asked Mr. Jackson what caused fog.

4. When a cloud is near the surface of the earth, it is called fog.

5. It is usually caused when a cold current of air from above strikes the moist, warm surface of the earth.

6. Mr. Jackson explained that condensation changes a vapor or gas to a liquid or solid.

7. The chill condenses the moist air into tiny drops of water.

8. These droplets are not big enough to fall as rain.

9. A large number of small drops absorbs more light than a smaller number of large drops.

10. Dense fog makes it difficult to see far, so traffic must travel slowly.

EXERCISE 2

Fill in the blanks in the sentences below with common nouns.

Saturday is my favorite day of the _____. I can either

jump out of my _____ early or sleep late. I usually get up at

eight o'clock in the _____ and put on my

_____ and _____. I eat

_____ for breakfast, brush my _____,

and comb my _____. My _____ joins

me. Together we play _____ and have fun!

List some things you play with in your free time. These items should all be common nouns.
Do not use names that have capital letters.

_____   _____   _____

_____   _____   _____

EXERCISE 3

Read each sentence below, locate the nouns that name a feeling or idea, and circle them.

1. Consideration for others is necessary.

2. My class is full of admiration for our school nurse.

3. Grandmother is always aware of my emotions.

4. Mr. Jackson has a thirst for knowledge.

5. My mother tells me to act with kindness to others.

6. Love for living creatures encourages me to be kind to animals.

7. In the summertime I enjoy my freedom.

8. My friends laugh at my silliness.

9. I play so long that only hunger brings me inside.

10. We have so much fun!

PROPER NOUNS

A noun that names a particular person, place, or thing is called a **proper noun.** Particular days are proper nouns as well. Proper nouns always begin with capital letters because they are specific names. If a proper noun is more than one word, capitalize all the important words.

Here are some examples:

PEOPLE	PLACES	THINGS	PARTICULAR DAYS
Leigh Buchanan	Peru	Liberty Bell	New Year's Day
Thomas Edison	North Pole	Ford Explorer	Groundhog Day
Sacajawea	San Diego Zoo	*Number the Stars*	Wednesday
Dr. Martin Luther King Jr.	Houston Astrodome	Scrabble	Grandparents' Day
William Steig	Grand Canyon	Red Cross	Mother's Day

EXERCISE 1

Rewrite the following sentences correctly by beginning all proper nouns with capital letters.

1. mr. and mrs. williams have traveled to many countries.

   _____

2. mr. williams met his wife, jolie, at the louvre museum in france.

   _____

3. They studied at oxford university for two years, from september through june.

   _____

4. On weekends, they explored all over england, scotland, and wales.

   _____

5. School breaks in july and august allowed time to tour many countries in europe.

   _____

6. jolie speaks the languages of italy and germany as well as that of her own country, france.

_____

7. After graduation, mr. and mrs. williams had a chance to visit hong kong, singapore, and beijing.

_____

8. Now, in the weeks before labor day, they take their motor home all over the united states and canada.

_____

9. They have made friends in many places, such as halifax, nova scotia.

_____

10. Their friend in halifax is a teacher at the atlantic elementary school.

_____

 EXERCISE 2

Mr. Williams received an e-mail message from his friend in Nova Scotia. The Canadian students wished to have American e-mail pals. Fill in information about yourself with proper nouns in case you might someday have an e-mail pal.

First and last name _____

City or town in which you live _____

Your state _____

Month or year born _____

Your school name _____

Places you've lived _____

Places you've traveled to _____

Favorite television show   _____

Best movie you've ever seen   _____

Title of a book you've enjoyed   _____

Favorite musical group   _____

EXERCISE 3

Underline the proper nouns in the following sentences.

1. In february we celebrate presidents' day for abraham lincoln and george washington.

2. We commemorate war veterans on memorial day, the last monday in may.

3. We carry our school flag and the flag of the united states on june 14th, flag day.

4. Our town—ridgewood, new jersey—has a big 4th of july parade every year.

5. Chanda's family went to philadelphia, pennsylvania.

6. She couldn't wait to visit a special science museum, the franklin institute.

7. Her parents took her to see constitution hall and the betsy ross house, where an early american flag was stitched.

8. Robbie went to visit aunt ann in baltimore, and they explored the national aquarium.

9. They also saw the fort where francis scott key wrote the star-spangled banner.

10. It was a warm summer evening when they went to camden yards to see the orioles play the yankees.

EXERCISE 4

Read the following paragraphs and decide which nouns are common and which are proper. Write them in the correct columns after the paragraph. Write each noun only once.

Long ago, the days of the week had no names. In those times only the months were separate. When cities were built, people wanted to have a special day on which to sell food and other items, a market day. The Babylonians decided it should be every seventh day. Other people kept every seventh day for religious purposes. In this way the week came into existence.

When the Egyptians and Romans adopted the seven-day week, they named the days after the sun, the moon, and five planets: Mars, Mercury, Jupiter, Venus, and Saturn.

We get the names for our days from the Anglo-Saxons, who called most of the days after the sun, the moon, and the gods of Norse mythology. The day of the sun was Sunnandaeg, now Sunday. Monday was called Monandaeg, the day of the moon. The name of Tiw, a god of war, led to our Tuesday. Wednesday was named for Woden, the supreme god in this mythology. Thursday's name is from the thunder god, Thor, and Friday is named for Woden's wife, Frigg, the goddess of love and beauty. The Anglo-Saxons kept the reference to Saturn for the day we call Saturday, originally Saeternsdaeg.

COMMON NOUNS   PROPER NOUNS

_____   _____

_____   _____

_____   _____

_____   _____

_____   _____

_____   _____

_____   _____

COMMON NOUNS	PROPER NOUNS
_____	_____
_____	_____
_____	_____
_____	_____
_____	_____
_____	_____
_____	_____
_____	_____
_____	_____
_____	_____
_____	_____
_____	_____
_____	_____
_____	_____
_____	_____
_____	_____
_____	_____

EXERCISE 5

Write a paragraph on the following lines. Tell what your favorite day of the week is and why you like it. Be sure to use both common and proper nouns.

_____

_____

_____

_____

_____

SINGULAR AND PLURAL NOUNS

Nouns that name *only one* person, place, object/thing, idea, or feeling are called **singular nouns.**

Here are some examples of singular nouns:

Our **class** loved *Sing Down the Moon* by Scott O'Dell.
We read this **book** last **month.**
It is about a **tribe** of Navajos.
Every **student** was impressed with their courage and emotional **strength.**
The **teacher** assigned a **project** so we could share the **story** with younger children.

Nouns that name *more than one* person, place, object/thing, idea, or feeling are called **plural nouns.** Most nouns change their spelling when they go from singular to plural.

Here are some examples of plural nouns:

Two **classes** are meeting to do research projects.
We have been reading **books** and writing for two **months.**
My group is doing a project on one of the **tribes** of Navajos.
The **students** in each group combine their **strengths** to make a good team.

These are six of the most common ways to make plural nouns:

1. Add *-s* to most singular nouns.

    myth**s**
    poem**s**
    fable**s**
    backpack**s**
    computer**s**
    goal**s**

2. Add *-es* when a singular noun ends in *s, x, ch, ss, sh,* or *z.*

    bu**ses**
    fo**xes**
    lun**ches**
    pa**sses**
    bu**shes**
    bu**zzes**

3. When a singular noun ends in a consonant followed by *y*, change the *y* to *i* and add *-es*.

fami**ly**	fami**lies**
sto**ry**	sto**ries**
ba**by**	ba**bies**
galle**ry**	galle**ries**
ci**ty**	ci**ties**
li**ly**	li**lies**

4. When a singular noun ends in a vowel followed by *y*, just add *-s* to make it plural.

t**oy**	t**oys**
monk**ey**	monk**eys**
vall**ey**	vall**eys**
b**ay**	b**ays**
turk**ey**	turk**eys**
rel**ay**	rel**ays**

5. When a singular noun ends in an *o* that is preceded by a vowel, add *-s* to make it plural.

ster**eo**	ster**eos**
rad**io**	rad**ios**
pat**io**	pat**ios**

When a singular noun ends in an *o* preceded by a consonant, add *-es* to make it plural.

ech**o**	ech**oes**
her**o**	her**oes**
potat**o**	potat**oes**
tomat**o**	tomat**oes**

There are some exceptions to these rules, such as *solos*, so check a dictionary to be sure of the correct plural.

6. You can make plural some singular nouns that end in *f* or *fe* by changing the *f* or *fe* to *v* and adding *-es*.

wol**f**	wol**ves**
hal**f**	hal**ves**
loa**f**	loa**ves**
wi**fe**	wi**ves**
li**fe**	li**ves**
kni**fe**	kni**ves**
sel**f**	sel**ves**

Some singular nouns do not follow a pattern—they are irregular. These special plurals must be memorized. Some are listed below.

ox	oxen
goose	geese
foot	feet
woman	women
child	children
man	men
die	dice
mouse	mice

EXERCISE 1

Rewrite each sentence and make the underlined words plural. Remember to make the verb singular or plural if necessary.

1. The <u>man</u> and <u>woman</u> went up the stairs at the same time.

   _____

2. The <u>student</u> drew on the <u>blackboard</u>.

   _____

3. The <u>artist</u> used oil <u>paint</u> on <u>canvas</u>.

   _____

4. Look at the <u>monkey</u> in that cage!

   _____

5. Grandma bought me a new outfit for the holiday <u>party</u> we're attending.

   _____

6. The bright <u>pattern</u> on the <u>couch</u> drew my <u>eye</u>.

   _____

7. My <u>puppy</u> came inside after running with me.

   _____

8. The <u>key</u> to the car got locked inside the trunk.

   _____

EXERCISE 2

Match the singular word in column A with its plural in column B. Write the plural on the line next to its singular.

COLUMN A   COLUMN B

fossil   _____   supplies

branch   _____   zeroes

supply   _____   gases

way   _____   fossils

child   _____   rays

seed   _____   branches

zero   _____   histories

history   _____   seeds

ray   _____   ways

gas   _____   children

EXERCISE 3

Decide whether each underlined noun in the sentences below is singular or plural. If it is singular, write S above the word. If it is plural, write P above the word.

1. Animals can communicate with each other by using signs and sounds.

2. When a mother hen makes a loud noise, her chicks recognize this as a warning of danger.

3. Dogs bark, lift a paw, or bare their teeth.

4. Animals know their "language" by instinct.

5. They make the right kind of expressions without ever being taught.

EXERCISE 4

Use the lines below to write a paragraph about animals. Underline your singular nouns once and plural nouns twice.

_____

_____

_____

_____

_____

_____

_____

_____

_____

_____

_____

_____

_____

POSSESSIVE NOUNS

Possessive nouns show a relationship between one noun and another. They show ownership—what someone or something has. To show ownership in a written sentence, we use a punctuation mark called an apostrophe ('). Look at the examples below:

The **cat's paws** scratched the table.

This is a simpler way of saying "The paws of the cat."
Who has paws? The cat.

The **players' shin guards** were still in the locker room.

This is a simpler way of saying "The shin guards of the players."
Who has shin guards? The players.

Luis's bicycle is black and green.

This is a simpler way of saying "The bicycle of Luis."
Who has a bicycle? Luis.

Here are the rules for making nouns show possession:

1. Add an apostrophe (') and an *s* to the end of singular nouns.

sun's	tennis court's
palm tree's	pool's
lifeguard's	tomorrow's
surfer's	

The **sun's** rays always seem hotter in Florida.
A **palm tree's** shade provides some relief from the sun.
The **lifeguard's** whistle is very loud.
The **surfer's** board was carried by the waves.
The **tennis court's** surface was made of clay.
A **pool's** temperature is usually refreshing.
Tomorrow's weather forecast calls for more sun.

2. Add an apostrophe (') and an *s* to a name to show that something belongs to a person.

Tami's   John's
Ms. Fernandez's   Mike's
Mr. Dunn's   Samantha's

All the girls in the class were invited to **Tami's** party.
There are many plants in **Ms. Fernandez's** office.
I returned my library books to **Mr. Dunn's** desk.
John's sister is getting married.
Ted admired **Mike's** baseball card collection.
Samantha's ring sparkled in the sunlight.

3. Add only an apostrophe (') when a plural noun ends in *s*.

parents'   pictures'
toothbrushes'   closets'
referees'   dogs'

The **parents'** meeting ended late.
Toothbrushes' shapes have become very creative.
The coaches were satisfied with the **referees'** calls.
The **paintings'** vibrant colors brought the images to life.
She lined her **closets'** shelves with scented paper.
The **dogs'** tails wagged happily.

4. Add an apostrophe (') and an *s* when a plural noun does not end in *s*.

children's   mice's
feet's   geese's
women's   men's

The **children's** pool has a diving board.
The **feet's** placement is important in this dance.
The **women's** track events took place in the morning.
The cat scampered over to the **mice's** hole.
The **geese's** migration takes place every autumn and spring.
My father plays on a **men's** softball team.

EXERCISE 1

Underline the possessive noun in each sentence.

1. Sunlight's white light is a mixture of all colors.

2. Have you ever seen a soap bubble's colors in the sun?

3. A child's pleasure in this discovery is heartwarming.

4. We can see the band of light's colors when it passes through water.

5. This band's name is a *spectrum*.

6. The colors' order is red, orange, yellow, green, blue, indigo, and violet.

7. The rainbow's beauty has inspired many people.

8. Aristotle, the Greek philosopher, thought a rainbow was a reflection of the sun's rays.

9. In fact, rainbows' curved spectrums are caused by light passing through raindrops.

EXERCISE 2

Rewrite the phrases below to make the underlined nouns show ownership or belonging. The first one is done for you.

1. the food of the <u>bees</u>　　　the bees' food _____

2. the nectar of the <u>flowers</u>　_____

3. the noise of the <u>hive</u>　_____

4. the flavor of the <u>honey</u>　_____

5. the sugars of the <u>nectar</u>　_____

6. the wings of the <u>butterflies</u>　_____

7. the changes of the <u>caterpillar</u>　_____

8. the web of the <u>spider</u>　_____

9. the activity of the <u>earthworms</u>　_____

10. the bite of the <u>mosquitoes</u>　_____

Now write three examples of your own using nouns that show ownership.

_____

_____

_____

EXERCISE 3

Write the possessive form of each noun in List 1. Choose a noun from List 2 to go with it.

LIST 1   LIST 2

1. furnace   _____   1. tap shoes

2. horse   _____   2. frame

3. dancers   _____   3. hard drive

4. candle   _____   4. heat

5. picture   _____   5. leaves

6. roses   _____   6. hooves

7. computer   _____   7. tires

8. tree   _____   8. flame

9. car   _____   9. erasers

10. pencils   _____   10. thorns

APPOSITIVES

Sometimes a noun needs further explanation or identification in a sentence. An appositive is a noun that is used to help identify or explain another noun. An appositive phrase is an appositive and other words that give more information about the appositive.

Notice that appositives are set off by commas if their meaning is not necessary to understand the sentence. When the appositive is in the middle of the sentence, a comma is placed on both sides. When it is at the end of the sentence, a comma is placed before it.

Look at the following examples. The appositives and the appositive phrases are in bold print.

I have two friends who can do yo-yo tricks. My friend **Claire** knows the most tricks.

Claire (appositive) explains who knows the most yo-yo tricks. *Claire* is not set off by commas because without this appositive the sentence does not make sense.

Ms. D'Alessandro, **a teacher's aide,** helped me with my math.

A teacher's aide (appositive phrase) explains who Ms. D'Alessandro is. *A teacher's aide* is set off by commas because the reader does not need this information to understand the sentence.

Our music teacher, **Mr. Chung,** sings in a rock band on the weekends.

Mr. Chung (appositive phrase) explains who the music teacher is.

Monopoly, **a game many people enjoy,** has been revised several times.

A game many people enjoy (appositive phrase) explains something about Monopoly.

My surprise birthday gift, **a mountain bike,** was hidden in the garage.

A mountain bike (appositive phrase) explains what the birthday gift is.

She spoke to Mr. Dunn, **the school librarian.**

The school librarian (appositive phrase) explains who Mr. Dunn is.

EXERCISE 1

Add commas to set off the appositives in each sentence. The first one is done for you.

1. Mocha mousse, my favorite dessert, is made with cream, chocolate, and coffee.

2. Lemonade a good source of vitamin C also tastes great.

3. Tacos a popular Mexican food are sold in the cafeteria.

4. Minestrone a vegetable soup is good on a cold day.

5. Beans and franks a New England favorite were traditionally served on Saturday evenings.

6. Colin's dad helped him make chicken tenders breaded and fried chicken strips.

7. Raisins dried grapes are often used in baking.

8. Last night Mom made succotash a mixture of lima beans and corn.

EXERCISE 2

Circle the appositive in each sentence. Underline the noun it identifies.

1. Thomas Edison applied many times for a patent, an agreement between the government and an inventor.

2. Daniel Inouye, a U.S. Senator from Hawaii, was the first American of Japanese descent to serve in either house of Congress.

3. Abraham Lincoln wrote the Emancipation Proclamation, a document that freed the Southern slaves.

4. Neil Armstrong, an astronaut, was the first person to walk on the moon.

5. Davy Crockett, a soldier from Tennessee, fought at the Alamo.

6. Ida Wells-Barnett, an African American journalist, helped to start the NAACP.

7. Franklin D. Roosevelt, president of the United States from 1933 to 1945, began several programs to help the poor.

8. Cesar Chavez, an American of Spanish-speaking heritage, worked to form a union for farm workers.

9. The inventor of the telephone, Alexander Graham Bell, tried until he succeeded.

10. Margaret Mead, an American anthropologist, studied life among the natives of Samoa in the South Pacific.

DIAGRAMMING POSSESSIVE NOUNS AND APPOSITIVES USING GRAPHIC ORGANIZERS

This section reviews how to diagram simple subjects and simple predicates and shows how to diagram possessive nouns and appositives.

Diagramming Simple Subjects and Simple Predicates Using Graphic Organizers

The simple subject and simple predicate are written on a horizontal line (_____). They are separated from each other by a vertical or up-and-down line (|) that intersects or cuts through the horizontal line.

Look at the sentence and its diagram below.

The teammates ran down the field.

| teammates | ran |

The simple subject is *teammates*. The simple predicate is the verb *ran*.
Notice that there is no punctuation.
Look at the next sentence, which contains a possessive noun.

Jenny's dog was groomed at the pet store.

The simple subject is *dog*, the simple predicate is *was groomed*, and the possessive noun is *Jenny's*. *Jenny's* describes or tells something about the dog. This is how to diagram those three parts of the sentence.

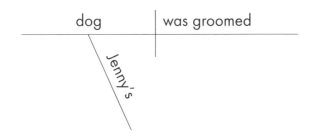

Here is another sentence with a possessive noun:

The woman's perfume attracted the bee.

The simple subject is *perfume*, the simple predicate is *attracted*, and the possessive noun is *woman's*. *Woman's* describes or tells something about the perfume.

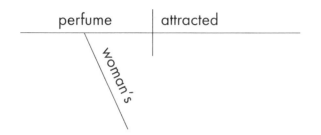

Look at the next sentence, which uses an appositive.

Caesar, my cat, runs through our neighbor's yard.

The simple subject is *Caesar*, the simple predicate is the verb *runs*, and the appositive phrase is *my cat*. *My cat* explains who Caesar is. This is how to diagram those three parts.

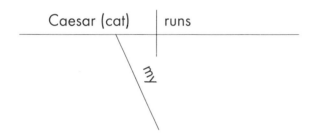

Look at the next sentence.

Cassie, the redheaded gymnast, is my best friend.

The simple subject is *Cassie*, the simple predicate is the verb *is*, and the appositive phrase is *the red-headed gymnast*. *The red-headed gymnast* explains who Cassie is. Those three parts are diagrammed as follows:

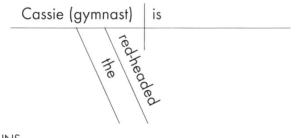

EXERCISE 1

Place the simple subjects, simple predicates, possessive nouns, and appositives in the graphic organizers below.

1. Carly will dance a solo in the recital.

2. We investigated crystals in science.

3. Harry Potter continues his adventures in *Harry Potter and the Goblet of Fire.*

4. Marni's bike rusted in the rain.

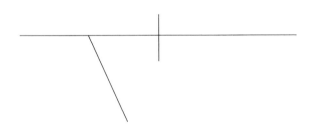

5. The teachers' meeting lasted until five o'clock.

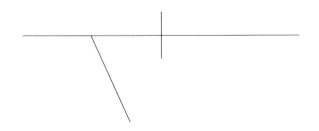

6. Megan's relatives arrived from Idaho.

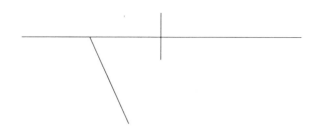

7. Hermione Granger, a friend of Harry Potter, studied for hours and hours.

8. Ms. Fernandez, the woman in the beige suit, is the principal of Christa McAuliffe School.

9. Myths, tales of fictional happenings, can have happy or sad endings.

Now write a sentence with an appositive or appositive phrase on the lines below. Then create a graphic organizer and write the simple subject, the simple predicate, and the appositive in the correct places.

_____

_____

_____

EXERCISE 2

Create graphic organizers for the sentences below. Write the simple subjects, the simple predicates, the possessive nouns, and the appositives in the correct places.

1. The relief pitcher, Cory Cheng, helped bring our team to victory.

2. Alyson's aunt is leaving tomorrow.

3. The circus has performed twice daily for the last two weeks.

NOUN REVIEW EXERCISES

REMEMBER: Nouns are words that name people, places, objects, things, ideas, or feelings. They can be singular or plural.

EXERCISE 1

On the line after each noun below, write whether it names a person, place, object/thing, idea, or feeling.

1. planet _____

2. dizziness _____

3. announcer _____

4. forest _____

5. attention _____

6. swing _____

7. aquarium _____

8. narrator _____

9. curiosity _____

10. thoughtfulness _____

REMEMBER: Common nouns begin with lowercase letters and name any one of many different persons, places, objects/things, ideas or feelings. Proper nouns begin with capital letters because they name particular persons, places, or objects/things.

EXERCISE 2

Rewrite each noun correctly on the line next to it. After each, write a P if it is proper and a C if it is common.

1. day   _____

2. tuesday   _____

3. patriot   _____

4. patrick henry   _____

5. seattle   _____

6. building   _____

7. world trade center   _____

8. month   _____

9. city   _____

10. september   _____

EXERCISE 3

Complete each sentence below by filling in the blanks with common or proper nouns. Your answers may be silly or serious.

1. On _____ my _____ will do something special.

2. Next _____ we are going to _____ on vacation.

3. The title of a _____ I enjoyed is _____.

4. I wish I could be a(n) _____.

5. This morning I packed my _____ and put some _____ in it.

6. When we go for a _____, we usually see _____.

7. _____ and I are planning a _____.

8. A state I'd like to visit is _____.

9. I feel _____ every time I finish my _____.

10. My _____ came to _____ from _____.

 REMEMBER: These are six of the most common ways to make plural nouns:

1. Add -s to most singular nouns.
2. Add -es when a singular noun ends in s, x, ch, ss, sh, or z.
3. When a singular noun ends in a consonant followed by y, change the y to i and add -es.
4. When a singular noun ends in a vowel followed by y, just add -s to make it plural.
5. When a singular noun ends in an o that is preceded by a vowel, add -s to make it plural. When a singular noun ends in an o preceded by a consonant, add -es to make it plural.
6. You can make some singular nouns that end in f or fe plural by changing the f and fe to v and adding -es.

Some singular nouns do not follow a pattern—they are irregular. These special plurals must be memorized. Here are a few:

man	men
woman	women
mouse	mice

EXERCISE 4

Write the plural form of each noun on the line next to it.

1. valley   _____
2. tooth   _____
3. self   _____
4. burro   _____
5. tree   _____
6. chef   _____
7. stereo   _____
8. church   _____
9. bookcase   _____
10. lady   _____

If the underlined noun is singular, make it plural. If it is plural, make it singular. Write the new sentence on the line under each sentence. Don't forget to make your subject and verb agree in number.

1. Spiders can be found in the <u>forest</u>, the <u>meadow</u>, and the <u>desert</u>.

_____

2. Their <u>bite</u> rarely causes <u>illness</u> to people.

_____

3. The playfulness of Geoff's <u>cat</u> always makes him laugh.

_____

4. Geoff's <u>collection</u> of miniature <u>cactus</u> still interests the cat.

_____

5. Even a cut on the <u>paws</u> does not stop the cat from investigating any new <u>plants</u>.

_____

6. What <u>trips</u> are you taking this year?

_____

7. My family visits Lakeside <u>Campground</u> every <u>year</u>.

_____

8. I have many guidebooks on the <u>shelf</u> in my room.

_____

REMEMBER: These are the rules for making nouns show possession:

1. Add an apostrophe (') and an s at the end of singular nouns.
2. Add an apostrophe (') and an s to a name to show that something belongs to a person.
3. Add only an apostrophe (') when a plural noun ends in s.
4. Add an apostrophe (') and an s when a plural noun does not end in s.

EXERCISE 6

Make each underlined noun show possession by adding 's or ' to the noun.

1. A scientist from the local <u>university</u> _____ science department came to our school.

2. The visiting scientist increased <u>everyone</u> _____ knowledge of lasers.

3. A <u>laser</u> _____ light is different from that of common light bulbs.

4. The <u>beam</u> _____ intensity concentrates the energy into a small area.

5. <u>Dr. Haas</u> _____ presentation explained how lasers are used to drill holes in diamonds.

6. <u>Colors</u> _____ effects influence people in different ways.

7. The effect of color can change depending on <u>people</u> _____ moods.

8. <u>Humans</u> _____ brains process visual information.

9. The <u>eye</u> _____ tricks are called optical illusions.

10. After the show we realized that color and light are no longer among <u>life</u> _____ mysteries.

REMEMBER: An appositive is a noun or noun phrase, often set off by commas, that further explains another noun in a sentence.

EXERCISE 7

Circle the appositive or appositive phrase in each sentence. Underline the noun it identifies.

1. Eleanor Roosevelt, President Franklin D. Roosevelt's wife, was a woman of many accomplishments.

2. Mrs. Roosevelt, a teacher and writer, also took on the role of official hostess in the White House.

3. The White House, the president's mansion, bustled with daily visitors.

4. Eleanor was First Lady during part of the Great Depression, a time when many Americans could not find jobs.

5. She helped increase support for the New Deal, a group of government programs developed to help people suffering from the Depression's effects.

6. During World War II, a war that lasted several years, Eleanor traveled widely through America as a fact-finder.

7. She later spent five years on the UN commission that wrote the Universal Declaration of Human Rights, a document that tells what basic rights all people should have.

8. Eleanor Roosevelt, one of the most famous and influential women in the world, is remembered as a role model.

REMEMBER: When diagramming, the simple subject and simple predicate are written on a horizontal line (_____). They are separated from each other by a vertical line (|) that intersects the horizontal line.

Possessive nouns are diagrammed on a diagonal line under the noun they refer to. The line goes from left to right.

Appositives are diagrammed inside parentheses immediately following the noun they refer to.

EXERCISE 8

Create diagrams for the following sentences and place the simple subjects, simple predicates, possessive nouns, and appositives on the correct lines.

1. The students wrote thank-you notes to the guest speaker.

2. Megan's dad jogged along with his dog.

3. The Johnsons, our neighbors, are an athletic family.

Now write three sentences of your own on the lines below. Then diagram the simple subjects, simple predicates, and any possessive nouns or appositives in your sentences.

1. _____

_____

_____

2. _____

_____

_____

3. _____

_____

_____

PRONOUNS

ABOUT PRONOUNS

Kyla likes to skateboard everywhere Kyla goes. Kyla wears a helmet and pads in case Kyla falls. Kyla's skateboard is red, yellow, and black. Kyla changes the colors of Kyla's skateboard every few months. Yesterday Kyla bought new wheels for the skateboard. Now the skateboard rides more smoothly.

Is there a way to make the above paragraph less repetitive? If so, how?

Replace some 'Kylas' with pronouns

Read this revised paragraph about Kyla.

Kyla likes to skateboard everywhere <u>she</u> goes. <u>She</u> wears a helmet and pads in case <u>she</u> falls. <u>Her</u> skateboard is red, yellow, and black. <u>She</u> changes the colors of <u>it</u> every few months. Yesterday Kyla bought new wheels for the skateboard. Now <u>it</u> rides more smoothly.

Notice that *Kyla* is used only twice. The words *she* and *her* were used to refer to Kyla. Although both paragraphs say the same thing, the second one is less boring and less awkward; it is not repetitious. *She* and *her* take the place of the words *Kyla* and *Kyla's*. In the same way, *it* stands for the noun *skateboard*.

Words that take the place of nouns are called **pronouns.**
Here are some other examples:

Tami took her soccer ball to school because Tami needed her soccer ball at after-school practice.
Tami took her soccer ball to school because **she** needed **it** at after-school practice.

The team members brought their practice jerseys so they could wear their practice jerseys.
The team members brought their practice jerseys so they could wear **them.**

Arjun told Grahame that Arjun would help Grahame with a project.
Arjun told Grahame that **he** would help **him** with a project.

Pronouns, like nouns, can be singular or plural. The chart below shows the singular and plural forms of the most commonly used pronouns. Begin to learn these pronouns.

Pronouns

	SINGULAR	PLURAL	EXAMPLE
FIRST PERSON	I, me	we, us	Use these to talk about yourself.
SECOND PERSON	you	you	Use these to talk about people to whom you are speaking.
THIRD PERSON	he, him she, her it	they, them	Use these to talk about other persons or things.

EXERCISE 1

Underline the pronouns in the following sentences.

1. This month we are learning about immigrants.

2. If they were headed for the East Coast, many immigrants first landed on
   Ellis Island, in New York.

3. Our teacher, Mr. Kaplan, said he would show us a film about immigration in
   the nineteenth century.

4. Mr. Kaplan's grandparents told <u>him</u> about being Russian immigrants.

5. <u>He</u> showed <u>us</u> a picture of <u>them</u>.

6. <u>It</u> was taken the day <u>they</u> arrived at Ellis Island.

7. Kelly has pictures of <u>her</u> great-grandparents the day <u>they</u> arrived.

8. Mr. Kaplan asked <u>me</u> to tell the class about Australia, <u>my</u> homeland.

9. <u>I</u> told <u>them</u> about the outback, the Aborigines, and the city of Sydney.

10. <u>He</u> said <u>you</u> could tell <u>I</u> felt great pride in <u>my</u> native country.

EXERCISE 2

Write the pronouns used to talk about yourself. Look at the chart on page 117 if you need help.

SINGULAR

_____ I _____

_____ me _____

PLURAL

_____ we _____

_____ us _____

Write the pronouns used to talk about people to whom you are speaking.

SINGULAR

_____ you _____

PLURAL

_____ you _____

Write the pronouns used to talk about other persons or things.

SINGULAR

_____ he _____

_____ him _____

_____ she _____

_____ her _____

_____ it _____

PLURAL

_____ they _____

_____ them _____

ANTECEDENTS PRECEDE PRONOUNS

Pronouns always refer to someone or something. The someone or something a pronoun refers to is called an **antecedent.** An antecedent usually comes before the pronoun that refers to it. The antecedent can be a noun or another pronoun.

In the sentences below, the pronouns are underlined.

Ted rode a bike to school. <u>He</u> locked <u>it</u> on the bike rack.

In the second sentence, *He* refers to the noun *Ted*. *Ted* is the antecedent of *He*. *It* refers to the noun *bike*. *Bike* is the antecedent of *it*.

    Look at the next two sentences.

<u>She</u> wanted to leave early for school. <u>Her</u> father offered to drive <u>her</u>.

In the second sentence, the first and second *her* refers to *She* in the first sentence. In both cases, *she* is the antecedent of *her*.

The antecedent can also be more than one word. It can be a combination of nouns and pronouns.

Matt and I are in the same class. <u>We</u> often study together.

In these sentences, *Matt and* I is the antecedent of *We*.

Gwen and Steve wanted to watch a movie, but <u>they</u> couldn't decide which one to rent.

Gwen and Steve is the antecedent of *they*.

EXERCISE 1

Underline the pronoun in the second sentence and draw an arrow to the antecedent.

1. Naoko spent an hour studying in the library. <u>She</u> wanted to do well on tomorrow's test.

2. Marcin's family is originally from Poland. <u>They</u> came to America five years ago.

3. Karim lives on Bedford Road. <u>He</u> walks to school when the weather is good.

4. Elise and I have played on the same lacrosse team for two years. We both
   hope to play in high school.

5. Mrs. Meyer and Mr. Sloan always arrive at school early. They have a great deal
   of work to do every day.

EXERCISE 2

Read each pair of sentences carefully. Label the antecedents in the first sentences by writing an A above them. The pronouns in the second sentences are all underlined.

1. Molly had never been to see a play. Her mother was taking her next weekend.

2. The actors spent time talking to the people in the audience after the
   performance. They wanted to make the audience feel welcome.

3. He and I practice pitching for hours every day. We want to be Little League
   pitchers this year.

4. The town library is open late on Thursday nights. It offers evening programs
   for senior citizens.

5. Mrs. Lonon spoke to Samantha and her friends about Aziza, the new student.
   She asked them not to treat her differently because of Aziza's disability.

   A pronoun must also agree with its antecedent in number. When the antecedent is singular, you must use a singular pronoun to refer to it.
   Here are two examples:

   My brother thinks he is a better speller than I am.

   (*Brother* is the antecedent; *he* is the pronoun. They are both singular.)

I will tell Alanna that she is invited to the party.

(*Alanna* is the antecedent; *she* is the pronoun. They are both singular.)

When the antecedent is plural, use a plural pronoun to refer to it. Here are two examples:

Tami bought the apples and gave them to Karl.

(*Apples* is the antecedent; *them* is the pronoun. They are both plural.)

Sara and Melanie like the children they baby-sit.

(*Sara and Melanie* is the antecedent; *they* is the pronoun. They are both plural.)

EXERCISE 3

In the blank, write the correct pronoun. Make sure it agrees with its antecedent.

1. Isaiah changed the channel to the show ___he___ liked best.

2. The students enjoyed watching the *National Geographic* special;

   ___it___ was an entertaining show.

3. I don't like this TV show because ___it___ is too violent.

4. The actor wondered if ___he___ would get to star in the new show.

5. Elaine sold the script ___she___ had written.

6. The plot was exciting because ___it___ had a great deal of action.

7. The comedians decided that ___they___ liked the story even though it was a drama.

8. The conceited director thinks that ___she___ is one of the finest film-makers ever.

You have learned that pronouns take the place of nouns and that pronouns have antecedents or words to which they refer. Now let's look at some groups of pronouns and the jobs they perform.

SUBJECT PRONOUNS

A pronoun takes the place of a noun; it can be used as the subject of a sentence. Remember that a subject tells who or what the sentence is about. A **subject pronoun** precedes (comes before) the action verb or linking verb.

Only subject pronouns can substitute for nouns as subjects of sentences. These are the subject pronouns:

SINGULAR	PLURAL
I	we
you	you
he, she, it	they

Here are some examples of noun and pronoun subjects. The subject pronouns are in bold.

Ms. Patel planned a trip to Nepal.
She planned a trip to Nepal.

Coach Fischetti referees on weekends.
He referees on weekends.

Ms. Fernandez and her secretary greeted the new students.
They greeted the new students.

The custodian and I helped the frightened bird to escape.
We helped the frightened bird to escape.

Here are some more examples of pronoun subjects:

I am happy that you are here.
You always enjoyed her singing.

EXERCISE 1

Underline the subject pronouns in each sentence.

1. We read about Rosa Parks in social studies.

2. She was a brave woman.

3. You know that she would not give up her seat in a segregated bus.

4. These days, it is hard to believe <u>she</u> was arrested for that!

5. When other people heard her story, <u>they</u> were angry.

6. In class <u>I</u> learned that the bus boycott was successful.

7. <u>We</u> are glad that Rosa Parks stood up for her rights.

EXERCISE 2

Decide which subject pronoun could take the place of the underlined word or words in each sentence. Write it on the line next to each number.

1. _____They_____ <u>Kyle and Tyler</u> took turns playing left wing.

2. _____It_____ <u>The book</u> was found under her seat.

3. _____We_____ <u>Ravi and I</u> were born in New Delhi, India.

4. _____He_____ <u>Dad</u> said we could stay up late tonight.

5. _____he_____ <u>Keesha</u> knows so much about history!

6. _____You_____ <u>Adam and you</u> can listen to my CD after school.

7. _____It_____ <u>The notebook</u> fell on the ground.

8. _____They_____ <u>The acrobats</u> flew through the air!

OBJECT PRONOUNS

Object pronouns follow action verbs and answer the question, "Whom or what?" These pronouns, like other pronouns, take the place of nouns.

SINGULAR	PLURAL
me	us
you	you
him, her, it	them

Notice that *you* and *it* are the same whether they are used as subject pronouns or object pronouns.

Here are some examples of object pronouns in sentences. The object pronouns are in bold.

Ms. Ravitz told the students.   action verb/noun
Ms. Ravitz told **them.**   action verb/object pronoun

Molly asked Naoko to come over.   action verb/noun
Molly asked **her** to come over.   action verb/object pronoun

I fed my gerbil.   action verb/noun
I fed **it.**   action verb/object pronoun

EXERCISE 1

Choose an object pronoun from the list above to follow the action verb in each sentence below.

1. Casey sent _____them_____ a postcard from California.

2. Ari helped _____him_____ fix his bicycle tire.

3. I learned _____it_____ after two hours of studying.

4. The teacher called _____me_____ on the phone.

5. My mother planted _____it_____ in front of the shrubs.

EXERCISE 2

Underline the correct pronoun in each of the following sentences.

1. Tisha's mom planned a skating party for (she, her).

2. Tisha spoke to (I, me) about her party.

3. She was inviting all of (us, we).

4. Mrs. Jackson took Tisha and (me, I) in her car.

5. Lori's dad said he would drive (they, them).

6. She gave (him, he) directions to the rink.

7. We met (them, they) there.

8. Everyone gave (she, her) a present.

UNDERSTANDING AND USING SUBJECT AND OBJECT PRONOUNS

Remember that subject pronouns are used as simple subjects of the main verb or verb-phrase in a sentence. They may precede an action verb or a linking verb. The subject pronouns are *I, you, he, she, it, we,* and *they.*

Object pronouns are used after action verbs. These pronouns answer the question, "Whom or what?" The object pronouns are *me, you, him, her, it, us,* and *them.*

Both subject and object pronouns take the place of nouns.

Read the two sentences below and decide which one is correct.

Ms. Buchanan asked Elise and I to help.
Ms. Buchanan asked Elise and me to help.

The second sentence is correct because object pronouns follow action verbs. Here's an easy way to figure out which is correct:

Take the noun and the word *and* away. Would you say, "Ms. Buchanan asked I . . ." or "Ms. Buchanan asked me . . ."?

Look at another example.

Her and me said we would help.
She and I said we would help.

Take away "and me." Would you say, "Her said we would help"? Take away "Her and." Would you say, "Me said we would help"?

Thinking about these examples will help you use the subject/object rules to decide which is the correct pronoun.

EXERCISE 1

Use the subject/object rules to help you choose the correct pronoun in column 1. Then write it on the line.

1. we, us   Mr. Chung, our music teacher, had _____us_____ audition for the special chorus.

2. I, me   He chose ____me____ to sing alto.

3. him, he   Alyson asked ____him____ if she could sing alto with me.

4. her, she   Mr. Chung asked Mai if __she____ would sing two songs in Japanese.

5. we, us   He wanted ____us____ to sing songs honoring many different cultures.

6. them, they   Parents said ____they____ would help with the various languages.

7. he, him   Noel's parents taught ____him____ the words to a Russian lullaby.

8. I, me   Alyson and ____I____ practiced at my house.

EXERCISE 2

Replace the underlined nouns in the sentences below with the correct pronouns. Rewrite the sentences on the lines provided.

1. <u>Ms. Buchanan</u> brought <u>lunch</u> to school.

     She brought it to school.

2. <u>Ted and I</u> shot baskets with <u>Kelly and Keesha</u>.

     We shot baskets with them

           RIDGEWOOD GRAMMAR

3. The new computers were delivered on Tuesday.

They were delivered on Tuesday.

4. Elise spent her allowance on a CD.

She spent it on a CD.

5. The bookstore sold the books at a discount.

The bookstore sold them at a discount.

6. Rebecca's mother took Rebecca to the ballet.

Rebecca's mother took her to the ballet

7. Dr. Janet Grodstein is a surgeon.

He is a surgeon.

8. Is Alyson playing with Chanda and Molly?

Is she playing with them?

WRITING AND TALKING ABOUT YOURSELF

I and *me* are the pronouns you use when you refer to yourself. To use these pronouns correctly, you must follow the subject/object rules that you have learned.

I is used when you refer to yourself as the subject. It precedes action verbs or linking verbs. *I* is *always* capitalized.

Here are some examples:

I am a student.
John and I play soccer.
She and I shopped with our dads.

Me is used after action verbs. Here are some examples:

Mom took **me** to the dentist.
Tell **me** your name again.
Ray will visit **me** tomorrow.

When you talk about yourself and another person, remember the subject/object pronoun rules to help you decide whether to use *I* or *me*. Always name yourself last when talking about yourself and others, whether you use a person's name or a pronoun.

Here are some examples:

Hope and **I** go in-line skating.   **I** go in-line skating.
Tami skates with Hope and **me**.   Tami skates with **me**.
Tami invited Hope and **me**.   Tami invited **me**.

EXERCISE 1

Underline the words that correctly complete each sentence.

1. Our Scout leader taught (Robbie and me – <u>Robbie and I</u>) how to tie the required knots for a special badge.

2. (Cory, Ted, and me – <u>Cory, Ted, and I</u>) went sailing with Grahame's family.

3. (Kelly and i – Kelly and me – <u>Kelly and I</u>) listened to my new CD.

4. (John and me – <u>John and I</u>) played lacrosse.

5. Luis rode his bike with (<u>Mike and I</u> – Mike and me).

6. The three-cheese pizza was prepared by Megan and (<u>I</u> – me).

7. My sister, my brother, and (me – <u>I</u>) appreciated the gifts.

8. (<u>My friends and I</u> – Me and my friends) were impressed by her friendliness.

Write several sentences about an event or a day in your life that was special. Be sure to use the pronouns *I* and *me* correctly.

_____

_____

_____

_____

_____

_____

_____

POSSESSIVE PRONOUNS

Pronouns can show possession or ownership just the way nouns can. Pronouns that show possession are called **possessive pronouns.**

Look at the examples below:

The girls' locker room was tiled.	**Their** locker room was tiled.
Colette loved the room's color.	Colette loved **its** color.
Rachel left Rachel's bag in a locker.	Rachel left **her** bag in a locker.

Notice that possessive pronouns *do not use the apostrophe* (').

Begin to learn the two groups of possessive pronouns. One group is used in front of nouns:

my	**My** lesson was canceled.
your	**Your** last name means "garden" in Italian.
his	**His** parents were born in Greece.
her	Isn't **her** pitching incredible?
its	**Its** meaning was unclear.
our	**Our** tickets came on time.
their	**Their** community service project was a great success.

The second group of possessive pronouns is used alone:

mine	**Mine** is in the garage.
yours	**Yours** will arrive tomorrow.
his	**His** is my favorite.
hers	Those shoes are **hers**.
ours	**Ours** are locked on the bike rack.
theirs	**Theirs** is the most powerful team.

EXERCISE 1

Underline the correct pronouns.

1. We wrote (our, ours) stories in the computer lab.

2. Molly said that (my, mine) story had a good lead.

3. (Her, Hers) had a surprise ending.

4. Karim and Jill said (their, theirs) didn't need any more revisions.

5. (Our, Ours) writing teacher said she revises (her, hers) pieces many times.

6. "(Yours, Your) first draft is never the finished product," she reminds us.

7. The teachers in our school created (their, theirs) own guide to revising.

8. I will check your story if you will check (my, mine).

9. Our teacher's favorite expression is, "(Your, Yours) finished product is never finished!"

10. I never realized that a writing class like (our, ours) could be so interesting.

EXERCISE 2

Write a new sentence, replacing the underlined word or words with a possessive pronoun.

1. Megan's mother speaks four languages besides English.

   _Her_____

RIDGEWOOD GRAMMAR

2. They offered to give us <u>their gerbils</u>.

_____ theirs _____

3. My father and I watched <u>Grandfather's</u> plane take off.

_____ his _____

4. Adam asked to borrow <u>my skateboard</u>.

_____ mine _____

5. <u>Her costume</u> was the most unusual.

Hers _____

6. <u>Samantha's and my</u> project was displayed in the hall.

Our _____

7. The coach told me to use <u>your glove</u>.

_____ yours _____

8. Everyone clapped after <u>Karim's and my presentation</u>.

_____ ours _____

CONTRACTIONS WITH PRONOUNS

A subject pronoun will sometimes combine with a verb to form a new word called a contraction. A **contraction** is made up of two words with at least one letter deleted (removed). An apostrophe (') replaces the deleted letter or letters. (It does not show possession, only that letters have been removed.)

Remember that the subject pronouns are *I, we, you, he, she, it,* and *they.*

Begin to learn the contractions in the chart below. Use this chart as a reference.

SINGULAR

I + am = I'm
I + have = I've
I + will/shall = I'll
I + had = I'd

you + are = you're
you + have = you've
you + will/shall = you'll
you + had = you'd

he + is = he's
he + has = he's
he + will/shall = he'll
he + had = he'd

she + is = she's
she + has = she's
she + will/shall = she'll
she + had = she'd

it + is = it's

PLURAL

we + are = we're
we + have = we've
we + will/shall = we'll
we + had = we'd

you + are = you're
you + have = you've
you + will/shall = you'll
you + had = you'd

they + are = they're
they + have = they've
they + will/shall = they'll
they + had = they'd

Remember to use an apostrophe (') to take the place of the deleted letters.

EXERCISE 1

Write the contraction for each pronoun/verb pair.

1. it is   _it's_
2. they will   _they'll_
3. I shall   _I'll_
4. he had   _he'd_
5. you have   _you've_

6. I am   *I'm*

7. you had   *you'd*

8. we are   *we're*

9. they have   *they've*

10. she has   *she's*

11. he is   *he's*

12. we will   *we'll*

13. she is   *she's*

14. I have   *I've*

15. they are   *they're*

EXERCISE 2

Rewrite the sentences below, changing the contractions to the correct pairs of words they stand for.

1. She's leaving for practice.

   She is leaving for practice

2. I hope they've made reservations.

   I hope they have made reservations

3. We're planning to meet at the park.

   We are planning to meet at the park

4. I'm not sure how much he's done.

   I am not sure how much he has done

5. You'll find it in the garage.

You will find it in the garage

6. It's my favorite flavor of ice cream.

It is my favorite flavor of ice cream

7. We were sure we'd studied enough.

We were sure we had studied enough

8. Kyle said he's met the new student.

Kyle said he has met the new student.

PRONOUNS AND HOMOPHONES

There are three pronoun/verb contractions that students often confuse with their homophones when they write. (Homophones are words that sound alike but are spelled differently and have different meanings.)

_it's_ sounds like _its_

_it's_ means "it is" (contraction)
its means "belonging to it" (possessive pronoun)

they're sounds like _their_ and _there_

they're means "they are" (contraction)
their means "belonging to them" (possessive pronoun)
there means "in that place" (usually an adverb) or it is a word that can begin a sentence. (You will learn more about adverbs in Chapter 8.)

you're sounds like _your_

you're means "you are" (contraction)
your means "belonging to you" (possessive pronoun)

When you write a contraction, check to make sure you are using the right word by making it two words. For example, change *they're* to *they are*. If you use a possessive pronoun, such as *their*, make sure it is followed by a noun. For example: their house. Using the right word will help keep your writing clear for the reader. Remember that *it's* is *always* a contraction for *it is*. It is never possessive.

EXERCISE 1

Underline the word that correctly completes each sentence.

1. (They're, <u>There</u>) are twenty-six characters or letters in our alphabet.

2. (<u>They're</u>, There) arranged in a traditional order.

3. (Its, <u>It's</u>) common to learn the letters by singing the alphabet song.

4. (They're, <u>There</u>) are also plenty of colorful books that teach the alphabet.

5. (<u>Its</u>, It's) letters are either vowels or consonants.

6. (Its, <u>It's</u>) important to learn that several consonants have more than one sound.

7. (Your, <u>You're</u>) expected to learn the letters of the alphabet in kindergarten.

8. It is (<u>there</u>, their) that you first learn how to print the letters.

9. You also learn to write (<u>your</u>, you're) name.

10. (Your, <u>You're</u>) taught that (<u>your</u>, you're) name begins with an uppercase or capital letter.

11. Whether a letter is uppercase or lowercase, (its, <u>it's</u>) sound is the same.

12. Although (<u>there</u>, they're) are twenty-six different letters, (they're, <u>there</u>) are many more than twenty-six sounds.

EXERCISE 2

Choose the word from the Word Bank that matches the definition below. Then write the word next to the definition.

WORD BANK

homophone	it's
they're	your
its	there
you're	possessive pronoun
their	contraction

1. __possessive pronoun__   a pronoun showing ownership

2. __it's__   the combined form of *it is*

3. __contraction__   the combined form of two words

4. __there__   a word used to point out a place

5. __homophone__   a word that sounds like another word

6. __they're__   the combined form of *they are*

7. __you're__   the combined form of *you are*

8. __their__   a word meaning "belonging to them"

9. __its__   a word meaning "belonging to it"

10. __your__   a word meaning "belonging to you"

BALANCING PRONOUNS AND NOUNS

Now that you have learned what pronouns are, you must learn to avoid overusing them. Good writing contains a balance of nouns and pronouns to keep readers interested and remind them what or whom is being discussed. Read the paragraph below.

The Wright brothers, Wilbur and Orville, were the first people to build and fly an airplane successfully. They had been interested in mechanics since childhood. They started out as bicycle shop owners in Dayton, Ohio. After attending high school, they opened their business and experimented with unpiloted gliders in their free time. They researched and discovered that Kitty Hawk, North Carolina, had just the right spot for their experiments. There, in the early 1900s, they tested piloted gliders for the first time. After this, they used their ideas to design and build an airplane. On December 17, 1903, he made the first flight in an engine-powered aircraft.

In the above paragraph, the names of the brothers are mentioned once; *they* is used six times; *he* is used once. Look at the paragraph rewritten with a balance of both nouns and pronouns.

The Wright brothers, Wilbur and Orville, were the first people to build and fly an airplane successfully. They had been interested in mechanics since childhood. The brothers started out as bicycle shop owners in Dayton, Ohio. After attending high school, they opened their business and experimented with unpiloted gliders in their free time. Wilbur and Orville researched and discovered that Kitty Hawk, North Carolina, had just the right spot for their experiments. There, in the early 1900s, the Wrights tested piloted gliders for the first time. After this, they used their ideas to design and build an airplane. On December 17, 1903, Orville made the first flight in an engine-powered aircraft.

Notice the different ways you can refer to the Wright brothers. Go back to the second paragraph and circle all the terms that refer to the Wrights.

EXERCISE 1

Rewrite these paragraphs, replacing the pronouns that are used too often.

1. Samuel F. B. Morse developed an electric telegraph in 1837. He began experimenting with magnetic telegraphs about five years earlier when he was painting portraits in Boston. He was lucky enough to receive both technical advice and money, so he was able to conduct more experiments. He also invented the Morse code, which was used to transmit messages. He received a patent for his telegraph in 1840.

_____Samuel___F___B Morse developed an electric telegraph in 1837._____

_He began experimenting with them about_____

_____

_____

2. Mary Leakey, an archaeologist, made several of the most important discoveries about hominids, the people who evolved into human beings. At age eleven she saw the famous Cro-Magnon cave in France and became very interested in anthropology and archaeology (the study of humans and the study of the things they leave behind). She later married another archaeologist, Louis Leakey. She traveled to Kenya with him to work on digs. One of her most important discoveries was a set of footprints south of Olduvai Gorge. She could now prove that early hominids had walked upright about 3.5 million years ago, earlier than scientists had thought. She helped everyone to learn more about our ancestors.

EXERCISE 2

Write down two other terms you could use to refer to the following people:

1. Madeline Albright _____ _____

2. Abraham Lincoln _____ _____

3. Orville Wright _____ _____

SENTENCE DIAGRAMMING USING GRAPHIC ORGANIZERS

This section shows how to diagram subject, object, and possessive pronouns. Look at this sentence:

Grandmother hugged me.

The simple subject is *Grandmother*, the simple predicate is the action verb *hugged*. This sentence is diagrammed as follows:

grandmother	hugged	me

Notice that the object pronoun *me* follows the action verb on the horizontal line. It comes after a vertical line that sits on the horizontal line.

Here's another example:

Ari called him.

Ari	called	him

Ari is the simple subject, the action verb *called* is the simple predicate, and *him* is the object pronoun.

Look at the next sentence:

Your brother bakes great brownies.

The simple subject is *brother*; the simple predicate is the action verb *bakes*. *Your* is a possessive pronoun that gives information about whose brother bakes. It is diagrammed as follows:

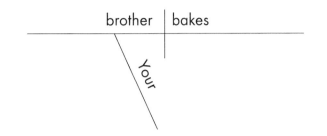

Here's another example:

My parents took me to the Grand Canyon.

Parents is the simple subject, the action verb *took* is the simple predicate, *my* is a possessive pronoun that gives information about whose parents, and *me* is an object pronoun. The sentence is diagrammed as follows:

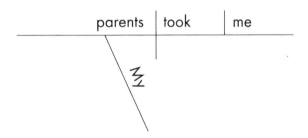

Look at the next sentence.

I found yours.

I is the simple subject, *found* is the verb or simple predicate, and *yours* is a possessive pronoun that stands alone. It takes the place of a noun and answers the question, "What?" Found what? Found *yours*. It is diagrammed as follows:

I	found	yours

Yours is placed on the graphic organizer like an object pronoun.

Here's another example:

She took mine by mistake.

She is the simple subject, *took* is an action verb that is the simple predicate, and *mine* is a possessive pronoun that stands alone. It takes the place of a noun and answers the question, "What?" Took what? Took *mine*. It is diagrammed as follows:

| She | took | mine |

EXERCISE 1

Place the simple subjects, simple predicates, and pronouns in the graphic organizers below each sentence. The first one is done for you.

1. He bought Mom a birthday card.

| he | bought |

2. Her present was wrapped in foil paper.

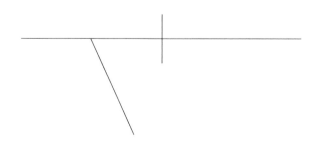

3. She tapped me softly on the shoulder.

4. Their parents scolded them for arguing.

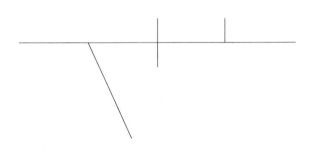

5. The teacher selected me.

6. We saw them at the playground.

7. Your team scored more points.

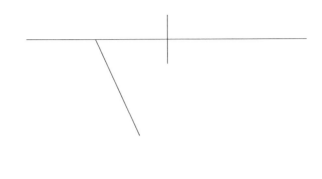

Create graphic organizers and write the simple subjects, simple predicates, object pronouns, and possessive pronouns in the correct places.

1. Our class stenciled on wood for Colonial Day.

2. Your goalie kept us from scoring.

3. Its mother was searching for food.

4. My parents gave theirs to a neighbor.

5. I love you.

PRONOUN REVIEW EXERCISES

REMEMBER: The most commonly used pronouns are *I, me, you, he, she, him, her, it, we, us, they,* and *them.*

Underline the pronouns in the following sentences.

1. The police chief did a series of presentations at our school.

2. He spoke about drugs, tobacco, and alcohol.

3. He explained the difference between legal and illegal drugs.

4. The teacher said that he was the most informative speaker she had ever heard.

5. I asked him several questions.

6. He began the first session by showing us a brief film.

7. It was interesting to learn about how tobacco was grown.

8. You couldn't help being concerned about the damage smoking causes.

9. Everyone said his presentations were great.

10. Many students said they hoped that the chief would come again.

11. Some of them asked if he could do a presentation on bike safety.

12. The day after his final presentation, we sent him thank-you notes.

REMEMBER: Pronouns always refer to someone or something called an antecedent. The antecedent usually comes before the pronoun it refers to.

EXERCISE 2

Underline the pronoun in the second sentence and draw an arrow to its antecedent in the first sentence.

1. Florence Nightingale is considered the founder of modern nursing. She introduced sanitary methods to care for patients and to clean hospitals.

2. Nancy and I love mysteries. We started a mystery book club at school.

3. Louis Pasteur was a French chemist. He developed the vaccine to help control rabies.

4. The license plate motto in North Carolina is "First in Flight." It honors the Wright brothers, who were the first to fly an airplane.

5. The principal's husband was a famous chef. He had won many awards.

6. Marie and Pierre Curie conducted experiments in radioactivity. They discovered radium, an element that was effective against cancer.

7. Venus Williams was the first black winner of Wimbledon since 1958. She is a talented tennis player.

8. George Bush and Bill Clinton were the presidents of the '90s. What an honor for them to be the last men to serve in the twentieth century!

9. "Paul Revere's Ride" is a famous poem about the American Revolution. It tells the story of how colonists were warned that the British were coming.

10. Her mother, father, and she arrived at the train station just in time. They had forgotten to set the alarm clock.

REMEMBER: A pronoun must agree with its antecedent in number. When the antecedent is singular, the pronoun used to refer to it must be singular. When the antecedent is plural, the pronoun used to refer to it must be plural.

EXERCISE 3

Write the correct pronoun that agrees with its antecedent.

1. The doctors had performed a miracle, for _____ had saved the man's life.

2. The girl answered the phone softly, because _____ didn't want to wake her baby sister.

3. The first team cheered when the teacher gave _____ an A+ for their project.

4. Mr. Johns, my next-door neighbor, left _____ briefcase on the train.

5. My project got wet on the way to school, and I had to do _____ over.

6. We decided to write _____ own jokes for the talent show.

7. Mr. Meakem baked tortilla snacks and gave _____ to Ari to bring to school.

8. Geoff and I live on the same block. _____ sometimes walk to school together.

 REMEMBER: The subject pronouns are *I, you, he, she, it, we,* and *they.* Subject pronouns precede (come before) the action verb or linking verb.

EXERCISE 4

Decide which subject pronoun could take the place of the underlined word or words. Write it on the line next to each number.

1. _____ <u>The teachers and the principal</u> met every Monday after school.

2. _____ <u>Mother</u> left for work each day before Dad.

3. _____ <u>Tyler and you</u> are invited.

4. _____ <u>Ms. Buchanan and I</u> edited my composition together.

5. _____ <u>Grandfather and Aunt Jane</u> helped Dad build my treehouse.

6. _____ <u>Mr. Fischetti</u> told us about his college days as a lacrosse player.

7. _____ <u>Ms. Patel</u> runs in marathons every spring.

8. _____ <u>My sister and I</u> cleaned the whole house on Mother's birthday.

9. _____ <u>The male peacock</u> spreads his magnificent feathers.

10. _____ <u>Ms. Buchanan</u> said, "Tisha, Molly, and you will present first."

REMEMBER: The object pronouns are *me, you, him, her, it, us,* and *them.* They follow action verbs.

EXERCISE 5

Rewrite each sentence below, choosing the correct object pronoun to take the place of the underlined word or words.

1. Our teacher taught <u>our class</u> about Christopher Columbus.

    _____

    _____

2. She said that Columbus convinced <u>Queen Isabella and King Ferdinand</u> to send him to find the riches of the East.

    _____

    _____

3. Columbus wrote in <u>his journal</u> every day.

_____

_____

4. The king and queen also wanted <u>Columbus</u> to help spread Christianity.

_____

_____

5. Columbus worried about his sons after <u>his wife's</u> death.

_____

_____

EXERCISE 6

Underline the correct pronoun in the following sentences.

1. The students wanted to surprise (she, her).

2. My aunt and uncle gave (I, me) a special present.

3. The whole family came to honor (they, them) on their anniversary.

4. The teacher gave (we, us) a due date for our project.

5. Ari asked (her, she) to spot him on the balance beam.

6. Can you drive Elisa and (me, I) to the party?

7. (Us, we) students think the plan is a good one.

REMEMBER: Subject pronouns precede (come before) action verbs or linking verbs. Object pronouns follow action verbs. Use the subject/object rules to help you choose which pronoun to use.

EXERCISE 7

Replace the underlined nouns in the sentences below with the correct pronouns. Rewrite the sentences on the lines provided.

1. In the Middle Ages, <u>children's</u> lives were quite different from those of kids today.

   _____

   _____

2. When boys from noble families were about seven, <u>the boys</u> might begin training for <u>knighthood</u>.

   _____

   _____

3. First, the boys became pages and served <u>the knights</u> at their feasts.

   _____

   _____

4. <u>A knight</u> had to have many skills.

   _____

   _____

5. A girl could become an apprentice and learn new skills when <u>the girl</u> was about twelve or fourteen.

_____

_____

6. If <u>the girls'</u> families were noble, <u>the girls</u> usually learned how to manage money and run a household.

_____

_____

7. If <u>the boys and girls</u> came from families that worked in trades such as weaving, <u>the children</u> had fewer opportunities to go to school.

_____

_____

8. <u>Young people</u> often learned <u>a trade</u> by working for a master.

_____

_____

9. Some of <u>the boys</u> learned <u>blacksmithing</u>.

_____

_____

10. Some of <u>the girls</u> learned to bake or weave cloth.

_____

_____

EXERCISE 8

Circle the correct pronoun in parentheses.

1. Ms. Buchanan taught (us, we) about plant life.

2. (She, Her) explained a process called photosynthesis.

3. (Us, We) asked many questions of (she, her).

4. Karim asked (her, she) if (her, she) could explain it again.

5. "Photosynthesis provides oxygen for most organisms, including (we, us)," (her, she) said.

6. Through this process, plants produce more food than (they, them) need.

7. "Do (we, us) produce this, too?" asked Noel.

8. (She, Her) gave (he, him) a long answer and showed all of (we, us) some illustrations.

9. Our assignment was to copy and label (they, them).

10. My favorite time in science is when (I, me) get to draw.

REMEMBER: Always name yourself last when talking about yourself and others.

EXERCISE 9

In the blank, write the pronoun that correctly completes each sentence.

1. My relatives and _____ celebrate Greek Christmas every January.

2. Karim and _____ celebrate our birthdays together.

3. My parents and _____ think celebrations are important.

4. When my class and _____ celebrated St. Patrick's Day, Colette and _____ wore green wigs.

5. Tami asked my sister and _____ how we celebrated New Year's.

Write several sentences about a favorite holiday that you celebrate with your family. Be sure to use the pronouns *I* and *me* correctly.

_____

_____

_____

_____

_____

_____

_____

_____

_____

_____

_____

_____

_____

_____

_____

REMEMBER: Possessive pronouns show ownership without an apostrophe (').

EXERCISE 11

Underline the correct pronouns.

1. Which one is (your, yours)?

2. (Her, Hers) sweater was hand knit by (hers, her) aunt.

3. (My, Mine) parents are celebrating (theirs, their) anniversary.

4. (It's, Its) coat was shiny and healthy-looking.

5. I gave (his, him) book back to (his, him).

6. I couldn't find (my, mine).

7. We studied using (her, hers) notes and (my, mine).

8. The teacher expressed (her, hers) opinion about the movie.

9. She was interested in hearing (our, ours).

10. We left (ours, our) wet boots on the porch.

11. (Yours, Your) handwriting is similar to (me, mine).

12. (Theirs, There's) is different from the others.

REMEMBER: In a contraction, an apostrophe (') replaces the deleted letter or letters.

EXERCISE 12

Write the contraction for each pronoun/verb pair; then use the contraction in a sentence of your own.

1. he is _____

2. it is _____

3. she had _____

4. they have _____

5. you are _____

6. we were   _____

7. I am   _____

8. they are   _____

9. he will   _____

10. we have   _____

 REMEMBER: Homophones are words that sound alike but have different spelling and meanings. These are the three pronoun/verb contractions and their homophones:

its	it's	
your	you're	
there	they're	their

EXERCISE 13

Circle the word that correctly completes each sentence.

1. (There, They're) have been many movie versions of *A Christmas Carol*.

2. Charles Dickens wrote the book upon which (their, they're) all based.

3. (Its, It's) about a miserly old man who learns the most important lesson of his life on Christmas Eve.

4. (You're, Your) certain to love (its, it's) drama and heartwarming ending.

5. The main character, Ebenezer Scrooge, is visited by three ghosts, each on a mission to do (its, it's) job.

6. (Their, There) missions are to get him to change his ways.

7. (You're, Your) introduced to the Ghosts of Christmas Past, Christmas Present, and Christmas Future.

8. (They're, There) not really scary when you realize that (they're, their) only (they're, there) to help.

9. (It's, Its) on TV every year in December.

10. (Your, You're) sure to find it in (your, you're) local TV guide.

REMEMBER: Good writing includes a balance between nouns and pronouns. Do not overuse pronouns in speech or writing.

EXERCISE 14

Rewrite this paragraph, replacing the pronouns that are used too often.

Michelangelo Buonarroti was an artist who lived in the 15th and 16th centuries. He was born in 1475, and he lived to be 89 years old. He painted and sculpted, he was an architect, and he wrote poetry. He had studied human anatomy, which helped to make him a master sculptor. He was totally absorbed in all aspects of his work. He was concerned about the people around him, and he had a deep understanding of the human spirit.

REMEMBER: The simple subject and simple predicate are diagrammed on a horizontal line separated by a vertical line that intersects it.

A possessive pronoun used before a noun subject is placed on a diagonal line from left to right under the subject.

A possessive pronoun that follows a verb and stands alone is placed on the same line as the verb, but after a vertical line.

An object pronoun that follows a verb in a sentence also follows it in a diagram. The pronoun and verb are separated by a vertical line.

EXERCISE 15

Create graphic organizers and place simple subjects, simple predicates, and pronouns in the correct places.

1. I biked to school with Cory.

2. Your homework fell onto the ground.

3. Ours is a close friendship.

4. Our teacher praised us for good manners.

5. She canceled the appointment.

6. His friends applauded him.

7. Their dog approached me.

8. My report was very long.

PREPOSITIONS

ABOUT PREPOSITIONS

Prepositions are words that connect one or more words to other words in a sentence. They help give more information about something else in the sentence. They are always written or spoken in a group of words called the **prepositional phrase.** The preposition is first, and it's followed by its **object,** the noun or pronoun that ends the prepositional phrase.

These are some of the prepositions:

about	behind	from	over
above	below	in	past
across	beneath	inside	through
after	between	into	throughout
against	beside	near	to
along	beyond	of	toward
among	by	off	under
around	down	on	up
at	during	onto	with
before	for	outside	without

You should begin to memorize these prepositions. Many people find that they can set the prepositions to a song, which makes them much easier to remember.

NOUNS AS OBJECTS

Here are some examples of prepositional phrases with a noun as the object of the preposition.

	Preposition	Noun object
We walked	**along**	**the path.**

Along the path answers the question, "Where?"

	Preposition	Noun object
She arrived	**after**	**the bell.**

After the bell answers the question, "When?"

	Preposition	Noun object
A glider can fly	**without**	**an engine.**

Without an engine answers the question, "How?"

	Preposition	Noun object
The girl	**in**	**the green jacket** is my sister.

In the green jacket answers the question, "Which one?"

	Preposition	Noun object
They formed a team	**of**	**sixteen players.**

Of sixteen players answers the question, "How many?"

	Preposition	Noun object
My dad made a stir-fry	**with**	**garlic and ginger.**

With garlic and ginger answers the question, "What kind?"

EXERCISE 1

Underline the prepositions in the following sentences.

1. Javier and Elena ran along the beach.

2. I walked through the doorway.

3. The team in yellow jerseys is the strongest.

4. Leo's dream vacation is a cruise around the world.

5. A package was delivered on our doorstep.

6. An octopus is a creature with eight legs.

7. We are studying prisms in science class.

8. The family chatted happily during dinner.

9. She ran for an hour.

10. Milena likes to get plenty of sleep the night before a test.

EXERCISE 2

In each sentence below, the prepositional phrase is underlined. Above each preposition, write the letter P; above each object, write the letter O.

1. She was sitting at the computer.

2. The man in the jogging suit is my uncle.

3. I hung my coat on a hook.

4. The principal spoke into the microphone.

5. Our school has many doors with six windowpanes.

6. Walk toward the fire station and then turn right.

PRONOUNS AS OBJECTS

Object pronouns are the only type of pronouns you may use after a preposition.

REMEMBER: These are the object pronouns:

SINGULAR	PLURAL
me	us
you	you
him	them
her	
it	

Here are some examples of prepositional phrases using a pronoun as the object of the preposition.

We ate dinner **with her.**

With her tells with whom we ate dinner.

Colette spoke **to me.**

To me tells to whom Colette spoke.

I bought it **for you.**

For you tells for whom it was bought.

Her parents sat **near them.**

Near them tells where her parents sat.

My aunt walked **between us.**

Between us tells where my aunt walked.

The toddler ran **toward him.**

Toward him tells where the toddler ran.

EXERCISE 1

Circle the prepositions in the following sentences.

1. We sang with them.

2. Ari ran behind him.

3. The girls left without her.

4. I had a sad feeling inside me.

5. The storm raged around us.

6. Tami would not go beyond it.

7. John will speak after you.

8. He received a letter from them.

EXERCISE 2

On the line in each sentence, write an object pronoun to follow the underlined preposition.

1. Molly spoke <u>to</u> _____ during lunch.

2. My parents went <u>with</u> _____ to the talent show.

3. Jill bought a scarf <u>for</u> _____.

4. She gave the tickets <u>to</u> _____.

5. Samantha and Lisa skated <u>with</u> _____ at the rink.

For each of the object pronouns, write a sentence of your own that uses the pronoun as the object of a preposition. Refer to the list of prepositions on page 158 if you need to.

_____

_____

_____

_____

_____

_____

_____

_____

SENTENCE DIAGRAMMING USING GRAPHIC ORGANIZERS

This section shows how to diagram a prepositional phrase. Look at the sentence below.

The school band practiced during lunch.

The simple subject is _band_; the simple predicate is the verb _practiced_. _During lunch_ is a prepositional phrase that tells when the school band practiced. This sentence is diagrammed as follows:

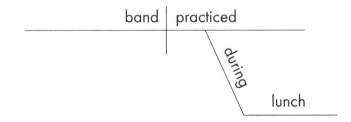

Here is another:

Ted ran to the park.

The simple subject is *Ted*; the simple predicate is the verb *ran*. *To the park* is a prepositional phrase that tells where Ted ran. The sentence is diagrammed as follows:

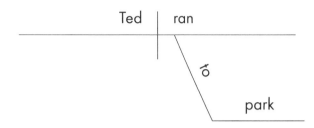

Here is another sentence:

The woman in the yellow car drove carefully.

The simple subject is *woman*; the simple predicate is the verb *drove*. *In the yellow car* is a prepositional phrase that tells which woman was driving. This sentence is diagrammed as follows:

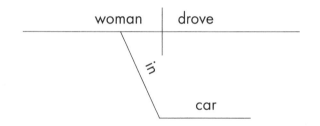

Notice that any adjective that describes the object of the preposition goes on a diagonal line from left to right under the object.

Write the simple subjects, the simple predicates, and the prepositional phrases from the sentences below in the correct places on the graphic organizers provided. The first one has been done for you.

1. We swam in the pool.

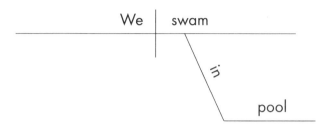

2. Sarah takes karate at the community center.

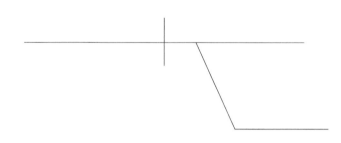

3. The car in the first space is ours.

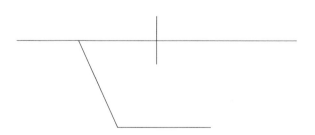

4. Milena handed the sweater to him.

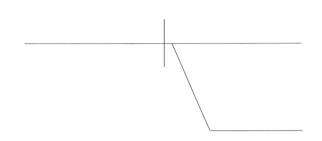

5. The people in the white house are coming to the barbecue.

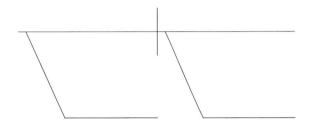

PREPOSITION REVIEW EXERCISES

REMEMBER: Nouns and object pronouns can be used as objects of prepositions. A prepositional phrase is made up of a preposition followed by a noun or an object pronoun. The nouns often have adjectives in front of them that give more information about them.

EXERCISE 1

Circle every preposition in the sentences below and draw an arrow to its object. There may be more than one prepositional phrase in a sentence.

1. Scientists use many methods for space study.

2. With the invention of the telescope, faraway stars, planets, and other space objects became visible.

3. A space probe gathers information about matter in space.

4. Scientists around the world work together to study the universe.

5. Astronomers are learning more about the history of the universe.

6. Mariner II flew past Venus.

7. The Mars Rover provided new information when it traveled across the planet's surface.

8. Other advanced instruments have been launched into Earth's orbit.

EXERCISE 2

Every prepositional phrase gives more information about another word in a sentence. On the lines provided, write the word (or words) that each underlined prepositional phrase describes.

1. _____ Rocks are made <u>of minerals</u>.

2. _____ There are three types <u>of rocks</u>.

3. _____ Igneous rocks are formed <u>from cooled lava</u>.

4. _____ Sedimentary ones are formed <u>by mineral deposits</u>.

5. _____ Moving water deposits the minerals as it flows <u>over the rock</u>.

6. _____ Sedimentary rocks are layered <u>in appearance</u>.

7. _____ Metamorphic rock is actually an igneous or sedimentary rock that has been changed <u>in a particular way</u>.

8. _____ These rocks are identified <u>by their special qualities</u>.

EXERCISE 3

Write a paragraph about a science topic that interests you. Underline all of your prepositional phrases.

_____

_____

_____

_____

_____

_____

_____

Place the simple subjects, the simple predicates, and the prepositional phrases from the sentences below on the graphic organizers provided for you.

1. The clouds in the sky will bring rain.

2. Samantha raced up the stairs.

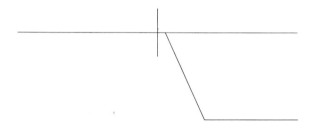

3. The teacher looked in our direction.

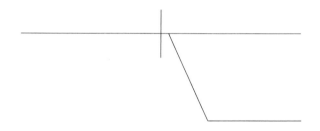

4. She turned toward me.

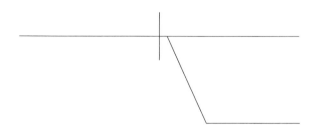

5. The team in the red jerseys walked onto the field.

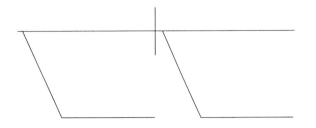

ADJECTIVES

ABOUT ADJECTIVES

An **adjective** is a word that describes a noun (a person, place, object/ thing, idea, or feeling). Adjectives give more information about a noun. They allow you to give a clearer picture of your meaning when you speak and write. In the English language, an adjective usually comes before the noun it describes. You may use one or more than one adjective to describe a noun.

Read the following paragraph and notice the underlined adjectives.

Alyson and her <u>older</u> sister, Melissa, share a <u>cozy</u> bedroom. As a <u>special</u> surprise, their parents told the <u>happy</u> girls that they would paint the room a <u>bright new</u> color. When the <u>entire</u> family went to the <u>paint</u> store, they found <u>many</u> choices. Finally they decided that a <u>turquoise</u> <u>blue</u> room would be <u>perfect</u>!

These adjectives describe nouns:

ADJECTIVE		NOUN
cozy	describes	bedroom
special	describes	surprise
happy	describes	girls

ADJECTIVE		NOUN
new	describes	color
entire	describes	family
paint	describes	store

What noun does the adjective *many* describe? _____

What noun do *turquoise*, *blue*, and *perfect* describe? _____

These adjectives limit the meaning of the nouns they describe: The adjective *older* limits the noun *sister*. Alyson may have other sisters, but this adjective tells us that Melissa is her older sister.

The adjective *bright* limits the noun *color*. It will not be a dark or a dull color.

Adjectives will answer one of the following questions:

What kind?
Which one?
How many?

In the following sentences the adjectives are in bold:

Dad and I chose **ripe** fruit.
He asked me to cut **this** fruit for dessert.
I combined **four** fruits to make a salad.

What kind of fruit? **ripe** fruit
Which fruit? **this** fruit
How many fruits? **four** fruits

EXERCISE 1

Write four sentences about your favorite book, movie, or TV show. Be sure to use at least one adjective in each sentence.

_____

_____

_____

_____

EXERCISE 2

Choose one adjective from each sentence and underline it. Then, on the line next to the sentence, write whether it describes what kind, which one, or how many. The first one is done for you.

1. Ben said he could not see <u>faraway</u> things easily.   _____what kind_____

2. His father brought him to a special doctor.   _____

3. Ben's far vision needed correcting.   _____

4. The eye doctor prescribed glasses.   _____

5. Ben tried on many frames.   _____

6. The large ones were funny on his face!   _____

7. A smaller size looked great.   _____

8. Ben and his father liked a lightweight pair   _____

   with oval lenses.

9. He calls them his super glasses.   _____

10. He is so glad to be able to see!   _____

EXERCISE 3

Draw a line under each adjective. Draw an arrow to the noun it describes. The first one is done for you.

1. Christa McAuliffe School has an <u>art</u> gallery in a <u>corner</u> room.

2. There is a colorful collage at the entrance.

3. Many shelves hold lovely pottery that students have made.

4. Unusual sculptures sit on round pedestals.

5. Twelve oil paintings in various sizes hang on the white walls.

6. Light from tall windows shows off shimmering watercolors.

7. Talented students folded bright paper into origami animals and hung them from the ceiling.

8. Pastel chalk drawings are kept in a glass case.

9. Natural and artificial light highlights the beautiful art.

10. Many visitors come and admire this collection.

MORE ABOUT WHAT KIND, WHICH ONE, AND HOW MANY

Do you ever see a picture in your mind? Try to create a detailed mental picture as your teacher asks you to imagine the following scene:

You are in your favorite place. What is it?
You may invite anyone to come with you. How many come?
What kind of day is it?

Which adjectives describe your favorite place? _____

Which adjectives tell how many are with you? _____

Which adjectives describe what kind of day it is? _____

Here are some examples of the three jobs adjectives can do for nouns:

WHAT KIND

quiet	quiet room
sunny	sunny day
green	green grass
intelligent	intelligent people
funny	funny clowns
warm	warm climate
skillful	skillful carpenter
active	active pet
bold	bold color

Adjectives that tell what kind give more meaning to nouns.

WHICH ONE

this	this protractor I'm holding
that	that evergreen tree out in the yard
these	these science projects in our classroom
those	those birds in the sky
first	first base
next	next showtime
last	last chance

This and *these* are adjectives that describe nouns that are nearby. *This* is used for singular nouns and *these* is used with plural nouns.

That and *those* tell about nouns that are farther away. *That* is for singular nouns and *those* is for plural nouns.

HOW MANY

one	one example
ten	ten dollars
two thousand	two thousand fans
five million	five million pennies
some	some soup
several	several crayons
few	few movies
many	many questions
more	more milk

Adjectives that describe what number may be specific or general.

EXERCISE 1

On the line after each noun, write a phrase using an adjective that tells what kind, which one, or how many. Then write a sentence using the phrase you created. The first one is done for you.

1. tree   that tree
_____

I love to climb that tree!
_____

2. airplane _____

_____

3. toy _____

_____

4. hamsters _____

_____

5. picnic _____

_____

6. dog _____

_____

7. music _____

_____

8. games _____

_____

EXERCISE 2

Decide what job each underlined adjective does and place it in the correct column in the chart that follows the sentences.

1. Corn is a <u>remarkable</u> plant.

2. There are <u>several</u> <u>general</u> types.

3. The <u>small</u>, <u>hard</u> kernels of popcorn explode when heated.

4. <u>That</u> type has moisture within the shells that turns to steam and pops.

5. <u>Sweet</u> corn may be eaten fresh on the cob, frozen, or canned.

6. <u>Pod</u> corn has each kernel enclosed in a <u>tiny</u> husk.

7. <u>These</u> <u>three</u> types of corn are among <u>those</u> species cultivated in the United States.

WHAT KIND	WHICH ONE	HOW MANY
_____	_____	_____
_____	_____	_____
_____	_____	_____
_____	_____	_____
_____	_____	_____
_____	_____	_____
_____	_____	_____
_____	_____	_____

EXERCISE 3

Circle the correct adjective for each sentence.

1. (Those, This) orange in my hand is juicy.

2. (That, Those) pictures you brought are sharp!

3. (This, That) rainstorm last week was drenching.

4. I want to try on (those, that) sneakers at the store.

5. The blue ribbon was given for (first, next) place.

6. Let's go to the beach (next, last) summer.

7. My favorite show was on (first, last) night.

8. (This, That) star shines brightly in the night sky.

POSSESSIVES AS ADJECTIVES

Like adjectives, possessive nouns tell which one. Remember that possessive nouns show what someone or something has. They give more information about the nouns they precede. They answer the question, "Which one?" or "Whose?"

Look at these examples. The possessive nouns are in bold:

The **dog's** leg was injured.

Which leg? The dog's.

The **sun's** rays are bright today.

Which rays? The sun's.

Han's father painted portraits.

Whose father? Han's.

I laughed at the **clown's** jokes.

Whose jokes? The clown's.

Possessive pronouns can also be used as adjectives that tell which one. Here are some examples:

His sneakers are in the hallway.

Whose sneakers? His sneakers.

Where is **your** house?

Whose house? Your house.

I lost **my** crayons.

Whose crayons? My crayons.

Her Web site has fun links.

Whose Web site? Her Web site.

EXERCISE 1

Underline the possessive nouns and pronouns in the following sentences.

1 Our music teacher sang with a local opera company.

2. The school's roof was being repaired.

3. Everyone said that his science project was the most creative.

4. T. J.'s father spoke several languages.

5. Yusuke's confidence soared when his class nominated him.

6. The hen's baby chicks were scrambling for food.

7. Many students buy their school supplies at the end of the summer.

8. Manina's birthday wish was to visit her grandparents in Spain.

A, AN, THE

A, *an*, and *the* are a special type of adjective. They are called **articles.** They signal that a noun will follow. These are the rules for using them correctly:

1. The article *a* is used before a singular noun that starts with a consonant sound.

   a car
   a video
   a snack
   a fort
   a house
   a unicorn

2. The article *an* is used before a singular noun that starts with a vowel sound.

   an apple
   an eraser
   an idea
   an observation
   an uncle
   an airplane

ADJECTIVES

3. The article *the* is used before singular or plural nouns that start with a consonant or vowel sound.

the kite (the kites)
the movie (the movies)
the swimmer (the swimmers)
the orange (the oranges)

A and *an* are used before singular nouns. Choose the correct one by the sound of the first letter of the word that follows it. If you are unsure whether to use *a* or *an*, it may help you to say the words out loud. Use *the* before singular or plural nouns.

EXERCISE 1

Write *a* or *an* on the line before each noun.

1. _____ explanation

2. _____ reason

3. _____ year

4. _____ aunt

5. _____ orangutan

6. _____ zebra

7. _____ swimsuit

8. _____ ice cream cone

9. _____ wheelchair

10. _____ envelope

EXERCISE 2

Circle the correct article in each sentence.

1. In 1790 (a, an) site was selected for (an, the) home of America's federal government.

2. Pierre L'Enfant designed (an, the) territory named Washington, D.C.

3. James Hoban designed and built (a, an) house for the president.

4. When (an, the) British burned (the, an) White House in 1814, (a, the) exterior was left standing, but (the, an) roof and interior were destroyed.

5. Rebuilding (the, a) White House in (a, the) same spot signaled that the U.S. government was permanent.

EXERCISE 3

Write a story with at least five sentences about the topic below. Underline each article you use.

Do you ever wonder what would happen if you were chosen to be the teacher of your class for a day? Write about what you would do and what rules you would make.

COMPARING NOUNS USING ADJECTIVES

Comparing nouns means telling how persons, places, objects/things, ideas, or feelings are alike or different. Adjectives may be used to compare nouns in three different ways. Read the following sentences and notice the words in bold.

A storm produces **heavy** rain.

The first sentence describes one thing, a storm.

A hurricane produces **heavier** rain than a storm.

The second sentence compares two things, a hurricane and a storm.

A monsoon produces the **heaviest** rain of the three.

The third sentence compares a monsoon to the storm and hurricane mentioned in the other sentences. In all, three things are being compared.
An adjective compares things in three ways:

1. To describe one noun: Today is a **hot** day.
2. To compare two nouns: Tomorrow will be a **hotter** day than today.
3. To compare three or more nouns: Friday may be the **hottest** day of all.

These are the forms we use for comparing:

1. To describe one noun: positive form
2. To compare two nouns: comparative form
3. To compare three or more nouns: superlative form

Here are some examples:

positive form:	A grapefruit is a **large** fruit.
comparative form:	A cantaloupe is **larger** than a grapefruit.
superlative form:	A watermelon is the **largest** of the three.

positive form:	This is a **quiet** class.
comparative form:	The class next door is **quieter** than this class.
superlative form:	The class at the end of the hall is the **quietest.**

When two nouns are compared, the comparative form of the adjective usually ends in -er. When three or more nouns are compared, the superlative form of the adjective usually ends in -est.

POSITIVE	COMPARATIVE	SUPERLATIVE
short	shorter	shortest
long	longer	longest

Below are some spelling rules that will help you use these forms correctly.

1. For adjectives of one syllable (and some adjectives of two syllables) that end in a consonant following a single vowel, double the final consonant before adding -er or -est.

POSITIVE	COMPARATIVE	SUPERLATIVE
big	bigger	biggest
red	redder	reddest
thin	thinner	thinnest

2. When adjectives end in a silent e, add an -r or -st.

POSITIVE	COMPARATIVE	SUPERLATIVE
simple	simpler	simplest
large	larger	largest
safe	safer	safest

3. When adjectives end in y following a consonant, change the y to i before adding -er or -est.

POSITIVE	COMPARATIVE	SUPERLATIVE
pretty	prettier	prettiest
messy	messier	messiest
funny	funnier	funniest

Most adjectives of two or more syllables form their comparative and superlative by using more and most. Never add -er or -est to these adjectives. Instead, use more for the comparative form and most for the superlative form.

POSITIVE	COMPARATIVE	SUPERLATIVE
helpful	more helpful	most helpful
wonderful	more wonderful	most wonderful
delicious	more delicious	most delicious

EXERCISE 1

Read each sentence, then circle the correct form of the adjective.

1. Andrew is a (stronger, strong) boy for his age.

2. His brother is (strongest, stronger) than Andrew.

3. Their father is the (strong, strongest) in the family.

4. A lake is (deepest, deeper) than a swimming pool.

5. What is the (highest, high) mountain in the world?

6. Jill thinks math is the (easy, easiest) subject in school.

7. My sister keeps her side of our bedroom (messy, messier) than I keep mine.

8. I am the (shortest, shorter) person in my family!

9. The class talked about my (favoritest, most favorite) book.

10. Of all the seeds we planted for our garden, the mustard seed was the (tiny, tiniest).

EXERCISE 2

The positive form of an adjective is in column 1 next to each sentence below. On the line in each sentence, write the correct form of this adjective.

1. cold   Where is the _____ place you've ever been?

2. fast   Tisha can run _____ than Lori.

3. helpful   Robbie asked if it would be _____ if he set the table or

              walked the dog.

4. few   John had the _____ mistakes on our spelling test.

5. wet   This is the _____ spring I can remember!

6. safe   Which is the _____ trail through the forest?

7. spicy   Mr. Williams likes spicy salsa, but Mrs. Williams likes hers even

              _____.

8. wonderful   Paul writes the _____ poetry in our school.

9. talented   Carolyn is the _____ artist of all.

10. funny   Tom is _____ than I am.

EXERCISE 3

Write the comparative and superlative forms for the following adjectives.

POSITIVE   COMPARATIVE   SUPERLATIVE

1. colorful   _____   _____

2. dry   _____   _____

3. fine   _____   _____

4. important   _____   _____

5. lucky   _____   _____

6. nice   _____   _____

7. serious   _____   _____

8. terrific   _____   _____

9. wide   _____   _____

10. young   _____   _____

IRREGULAR ADJECTIVES

A few adjectives change to different words when they form the comparative and superlative. These are called **irregular** adjectives and must be memorized.

POSITIVE	COMPARATIVE	SUPERLATIVE
good	better	best
bad	worse	worst
many	more	most
much	more	most

 REMEMBER: Use the comparative form when comparing two nouns. Use the superlative form when comparing three or more nouns. Here are some examples:

I have a **good** time playing video games.

I have a **better** time riding my scooter.

I have the **best** time swimming at the lake!

We had **bad** weather when we left on our field trip.

The weather got **worse** by lunchtime.

The weather was the **worst** by the time we got back to school!

EXERCISE 1

Underline the correct form of the adjective in each sentence.

1. I have (much, many) more homework today than yesterday.

2. Which of these two CDs do you think is (best, better)?

3. My old printer is (worse, worst) than Lisa's new one.

4. What is the (good, best) movie you've ever seen?

5. Khalilah has memorized the (more, most) spelling words of anyone in the class.

6. Rebecca did a (best, good) job playing shortstop.

7. The (bad, worst) luck for us was when the other team made a double play.

8. The famous chef received (many, much) requests for her recipes.

9. Colin had a (more, bad) cold, so he ate oranges for vitamin C.

10. The gardener planted (more, worst) seeds in the spring.

EXERCISE 2

Write five sentences that use the comparative or superlative form of the adjective (or adjectives) in column 1.

1. good _____

2. bad _____

3. many _____

4. much _____

5. bad, good _____

PROPER ADJECTIVES

An adjective that is made from a proper noun is called a **proper adjective.** A proper adjective is always capitalized, just as a proper noun is always capitalized.

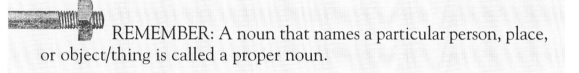

REMEMBER: A noun that names a particular person, place, or object/thing is called a proper noun.

Here are some examples of proper adjectives made from proper nouns:

PROPER NOUN	PROPER ADJECTIVE
North America	North American
Africa	African
South America	South American
Europe	European
Australia	Australian

Notice that when a proper adjective is two words, such as *North American* and *South American*, both words are capitalized. A proper adjective usually comes before the noun it describes. Here are some examples of proper adjectives that come before the nouns they describe:

Sicilian pizza
French fries
Turkish taffy
Italian bread

PROPER NOUN	PROPER ADJECTIVE
Sicily	Sicilian
France	French
Turkey	Turkish
Italy	Italian

Many proper adjectives are formed from proper nouns that name places.

EXERCISE 1

Underline the proper adjectives in each sentence.

1. Hawaiian pineapples taste delicious.

2. Suzy's mother taught our class how to make Chinese dumplings.

3. South American coffee is a popular export.

4. Sweaters made of thick Scottish wool are very warm.

5. The Australian outback is rugged territory.

6. European students learn several languages.

7. Kyle's grandma follows the English tradition of serving afternoon tea.

8. Early American furniture is different from modern Scandinavian furniture.

9. Mr. Williams ate a Greek salad for lunch.

10. Caesar was an early Roman emperor.

EXERCISE 2

Read the noun phrases below. Then choose the correct proper adjective from the word bank and rewrite the adjective phrase on the line next to each noun phrase. The first two are done for you.

ADJECTIVE WORD BANK

Jamaican	Egyptian	Belgian
Italian	Saudi Arabian	African
Alaskan	Swiss	Argentinian
Cuban		

NOUN PHRASE   ADJECTIVE PHRASE

1. cotton from Egypt   Egyptian cotton

2. mountains in Switzerland   Swiss mountains

3. pasta from Italy   _____

4. pottery from Africa   _____

5. cattle from Argentina   _____

6. icebergs in Alaska   _____

7. the desert in Saudi Arabia   _____

8. music from Cuba   _____

9. beaded jewelry from Jamaica   _____

10. lace from Belgium   _____

SENTENCE DIAGRAMMING USING GRAPHIC ORGANIZERS

An adjective is diagrammed on a slanting line from left to right below the noun that it describes. Look at where the adjectives are placed on the graphic organizer that follows this sentence:

A new student joined our class.

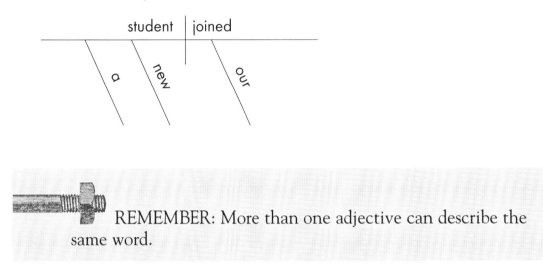

REMEMBER: More than one adjective can describe the same word.

The article *a* is diagrammed just like the adjective *new*. Place the words on the lines in the order in which they appear in the sentence.

Complete the graphic organizer for the following sentence:

The soft music played.

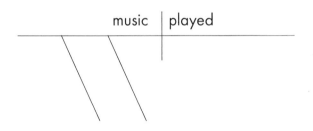

Did you place the adjectives *the* and *soft* on the slanting lines below the noun, *music*, that they describe?

EXERCISE 1

Diagram the following sentences by placing the simple subjects, simple predicates, and the adjectives on the correct lines.

1. The happy people danced.

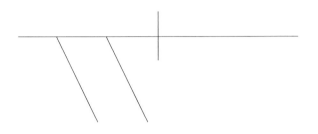

2. A large vase fell.

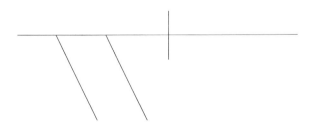

3. The frisky puppy ran.

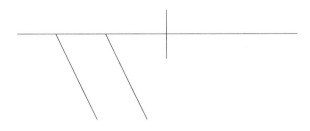

4. The popular actor waved.

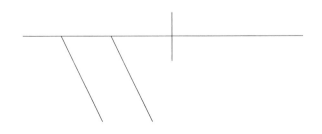

Sometimes an adjective follows a form of the verb *be* (*am, is, are, was, were*). The linking verb and its subject are diagrammed in the same way as action verbs. However, in a diagram with linking verbs the adjective is written on the same line as the linking verb. A line slanting to the left divides the linking verb and the adjective. The adjective that follows the form of the verb *be* is written on the horizontal line following the diagonal line. Here are two examples:

Television is entertaining.

Her hair was very long.

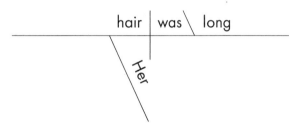

Notice that the line dividing the adjective and the verb slants backward toward the subject. Thinking of the line going toward the subject will help you remember that the adjective describes the subject.

EXERCISE 2

Place the simple subjects, the form of the verb *be*, and the adjectives in the correct spaces on the graphic organizers below.

1. I am thirsty.

2. That old watch is valuable.

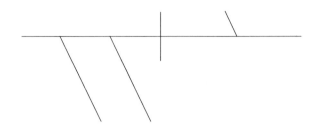

3. Karim is funny.

4. The tire was flat.

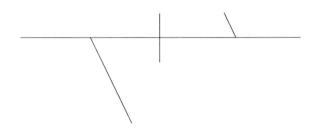

5. The circus animals were talented.

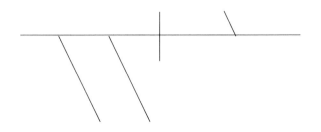

Complete the graphic organizers for the following sentences. Place the simple subjects, simple predicates, adjectives, and articles on the correct lines.

1. The Indian doll was beautiful.

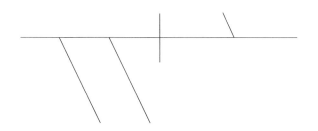

2. My sore throat is better.

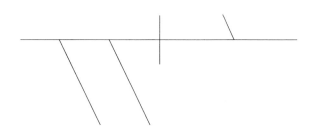

3. Our French teacher is Canadian.

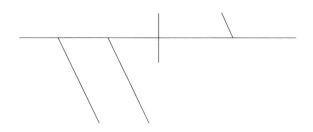

ADJECTIVE REVIEW EXERCISES

 REMEMBER: A word that describes a noun is called an adjective. It usually comes before the noun and answers one of the following questions: *what kind?*, *which one?*, or *how many?*

 ## EXERCISE 1

In the following paragraphs, underline all the adjectives that describe a noun. Do not underline the articles.

Dedicated scientists are studying the world's oceans to learn more about them. They have found that the floor of the deepest regions is made up of tiny parts of animals' skeletons, small plants, and volcanic ash. They form a rust-colored material called red clay. The deepest section is in the Mariana Trench, where the water's depth is nearly seven miles.

The depth of oceans can be measured by sending down sound waves that reflect back from the ocean floor. Scientists measure how long it takes for these sound waves to return to them, then divide this time in half. With today's technology we continue to discover more about the oceans that cover much of our earth's surface.

REMEMBER: The articles *a* and *an* are used before singular nouns. The article *the* is used before singular and plural nouns.

EXERCISE 2

Circle the correct article in each sentence.

1. Naoko went on vacation to the shore of (a, the) Atlantic Ocean.

2. She noticed on (a, the) windy days there were many waves in (the, an) water.

3. On (a, an) calm day there were few waves.

4. (A, An) type of energy must start (a, an) wave.

5. In (the, a) water, (an, the) wind provides that energy.

6. Water particles move mostly up and down in (a, an) wave.

7. They move in (a, an) circular path, pushed by (an, the) wind.

8. Near (the, an) beach, (a, the) bottom of (a, an) wave strikes (an, the) ground and slows.

9. When (the, an) top of (a, an) wave goes faster than (an, the) bottom, it forms (a, an) breaker.

10. Naoko learned to be very careful in (a, the) waves!

 REMEMBER: The positive form of an adjective describes one noun. The comparative form of an adjective compares two nouns. The superlative form of an adjective compares three or more nouns.

EXERCISE 3

Complete the following chart by filling in the missing comparative and superlative forms of each adjective.

POSITIVE	COMPARATIVE	SUPERLATIVE
1. bright	_____	_____
2. thin	_____	_____
3. safe	_____	_____

POSITIVE	COMPARATIVE	SUPERLATIVE
4. funny	_____	_____
5. beautiful	_____	_____
6. heavy	_____	_____
7. tall	_____	_____
8. helpful	_____	_____
9. hot	_____	_____
10. kind	_____	_____

EXERCISE 4

From the chart above, choose two adjectives in the positive form and use each in a sentence.

_____

_____

From the chart above, choose two adjectives in the comparative form and use each in a sentence.

_____

_____

From the chart above, choose two adjectives in the superlative form and use each in a sentence.

_____

_____

EXERCISE 5

On the line after each sentence, write the correct form of the irregular adjective in parentheses.

1. Your handwriting is (good) than mine.   better _____

2. In our class, Colin is on the (many) teams.   _____

3. The (good) amateur athletes play in the Olympics.   _____

4. I got the (bad) score of everyone playing that video game.   _____

5. Is it (bad) to feel too hot or too cold?   _____

6. Mr. Williams gave us (much) time to study for our test.   _____

7. Who had the (good) time for running the mile in your class?   _____

8. I like pasta (much) than rice.   _____

EXERCISE 6

Rewrite the following sentences correctly by capitalizing the proper adjectives.

1. The form of english writing is different from the japanese form.

   _____

2. Paella, a spanish rice dish, also contains meat, vegetables, and seafood.

   _____

3. The somalian flag has a white star on a blue background.

   _____

4. An american presidential election is held every four years.

   _____

5. An oil spill in alaskan waters was devastating to wildlife.

   _____

6. Michelangelo used italian marble for his sculptures.

   _____

7. The official brazilian national language is Portuguese.

   _____

8. A famous french museum is called the Louvre.

   _____

9. The south australian tiger snake may be the most deadly of all land snakes.

   _____

10. George Washington Carver was an african american botanist, chemist, and
    educator.

    _____

REMEMBER: When you diagram a sentence, the simple subject and simple predicate are organized on a horizontal line intersected by a vertical line. An adjective is placed on a slanting line from left to right below the noun that it describes. An adjective after a linking verb is placed on the same line as the verb and subject. A slanting line from left to right separates the adjective and the linking verb. A diagram does not have any punctuation.

 EXERCISE 7

Diagram the following sentences by placing the simple subjects, simple predicates, and adjectives on the correct lines. Be sure to include the articles.

1. The Statue of Liberty is impressive.

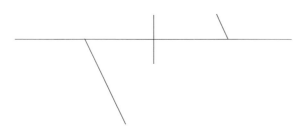

2. Forty-one Pilgrims signed the Mayflower Compact.

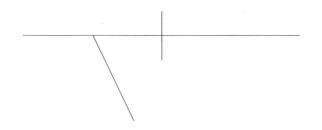

3. Tourist attractions bring many visitors.

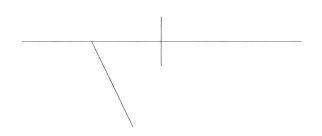

4. The fresh fruit was wonderful!

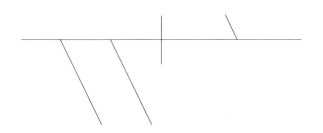

5. The three children played on the sidewalk.

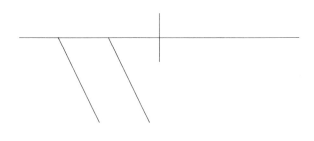

EXERCISE 8

Write three sentences of your own that have at least one adjective in them.

_____

_____

_____

_____

_____

Now create graphic organizers for two sentences of your choice from the three you have written.

1.

2.

ADVERBS

ABOUT ADVERBS

An **adverb** is another part of speech that can help you speak or write clearly. Just as an adjective tells you more about a noun, an adverb tells you more about a verb.

An adverb is similar to an adjective because it gives more meaning or detail to another word in a sentence. An adverb can come before or after the verb it describes. Which of the following sentences tells more clearly what happened?

Jill walked to school.
Jill walked rapidly to school.

In the first sentence there is no word that tells *how* Jill walked. In the second sentence the word *rapidly* describes how Jill walked. *Rapidly* is an adverb. It tells you more about the verb *walked*.

Adverbs often tell how, when, or where.

The plane landed **smoothly.**

How did the plane land? It landed **smoothly.**

Andrew skateboards **often.**

When does Andrew skateboard? He skateboards **often.**

Molly plays tennis **here.**

Where does Molly play tennis? She plays tennis **here.**
In the following sentences, the adverbs are in bold.

The sky is darkening **slowly.**
The firefighters responded **bravely** to the emergency.
Mr. Williams **carefully** explained the math problem.

In the first sentence the adverb *slowly* describes the verb phrase *is darkening*. In the second sentence the adverb *bravely* describes the verb *responded*. What verb does the adverb *carefully* describe in the third sentence? Write it on the line below.

_____

From the example above, you can see that adverbs are often formed by adding *-ly* to an adjective. Here are other examples:

ADJECTIVE	+	LY	=	ADVERB
firm	+	ly	=	firmly
strong	+	ly	=	strongly
neat	+	ly	=	neatly
loud	+	ly	=	loudly
proud	+	ly	=	proudly

When the adverb ends in *y*, change the *y* to *i* and add *-ly.*

ADVERB	+	LY	=	ADVERB
lofty to lofti	+	ly	=	loftily
sturdy to sturdi	+	ly	=	sturdily
angry to angri	+	ly	=	angrily
happy to happi	+	ly	=	happily

Sometimes an adverb has the same form as an adjective:

My father drove **fast** on the way to the hospital.
Khalilah held her dog **close** so he wouldn't be afraid of the thunder.
Ian came **late** to class today.

These adverbs describe verbs. If the words were used to describe nouns, they would be adjectives. Here are the same words used as adjectives:

The cheetah is a **fast** runner.
That was a **close** game!
We're having a **late** spring this year.

Here is a chart that shows some other *how*, *when*, and *where* adverbs.

HOW	WHEN	WHERE
well	now	here
fairly	then	there
skillfully	soon	up
cleverly	again	down
fiercely	today	somewhere

EXERCISE 1

Underline the adverbs in the following sentences.

1. The three mice ran blindly.

2. The cow jumped gracefully over the moon.

3. Jack and Jill climbed steadily up the hill.

4. Little Miss Muffet sat daintily on her tuffet.

5. Jack jumped nimbly over the candlestick.

6. The billy goat spoke gruffly.

7. Cinderella swept gloomily as her stepsisters left for the ball.

8. Peter ate his pumpkin hungrily.

Underline each adverb in the sentence below; then draw an arrow from the adverb to the verb it describes. The first one is done for you.

1. Michael and I went to the city <u>yesterday</u>.

2. We traveled comfortably on the commuter train.

3. The scenery passed quickly.

4. At last the train noisily pulled into the station.

5. People hurriedly left the train, but Michael and I walked leisurely.

6. We went directly to the museum with the West African exhibit.

7. Student groups were waiting excitedly outside the museum.

8. Michael and I gladly followed one of the museum guides.

9. Several people politely asked questions.

10. I smiled proudly as the guide told about the customs of my ancestors.

EXERCISE 3

In each sentence below, the adverb is underlined and an arrow points to the verb it describes. Decide whether the adverb answers *how, where,* or *when,* and write *how, where,* or *when* on the line in front of the sentence. The first one is done for you.

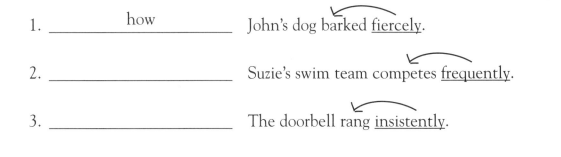

1. _____how_____ John's dog barked <u>fiercely</u>.

2. _____ Suzie's swim team competes <u>frequently</u>.

3. _____ The doorbell rang <u>insistently</u>.

4. _____ Exercise <u>regularly</u> and improve your health.

5. _____ I put my backpack <u>somewhere</u>, but I can't remember where.

6. _____ My mother <u>sometimes</u> pitches at my practice sessions.

ADVERBS WITH ADJECTIVES

Adverbs can describe adjectives as well as verbs. *Very* is one of the most common adverbs used in this way.

> Saturday was a very hot day.
> The science test was tremendously hard.
> The music at the restaurant was annoyingly loud.
> I was very surprised to receive a package.

Be careful not to overuse *very*. You can often find a livelier adjective that describes what you want to say better than "very fun," "very bad," "very good," and so on.

COMPARING WITH ADVERBS

Adverbs, like adjectives, can be used to make comparisons using three different forms: positive, comparative, and superlative. **Positive** describes something but does not compare it with anything else, **comparative** compares two things or people, and **superlative** compares more than two things or people.

These adverb forms also have spelling patterns. Most one-syllable adverbs and some two-syllable adverbs add *-er* to form the comparative and *-est* to form the superlative. When the adverb ends in *-y*, change the *-y* to *-i* and add *-er* or *-est*. Here are some examples:

POSITIVE	COMPARATIVE	SUPERLATIVE
hard	harder	hardest
near	nearer	nearest
early	earlier	earliest
soon	sooner	soonest

Most of the time, when adverbs end in -*ly* we use the words *more* and *most* to form their comparative and superlative forms. Never add -*er* or -*est* to these adverbs. Instead, use *more* in front of the adverb for the comparative form and *most* in front of the adverb for the superlative form. Here are some examples:

POSITIVE	COMPARATIVE	SUPERLATIVE
quickly	more quickly	most quickly
frequently	more frequently	most frequently
smoothly	more smoothly	most smoothly
carefully	more carefully	most carefully

There is a small group of irregular adverbs. They form their comparative and superlative forms by changing the words. These adverbs must be memorized in their three forms.

POSITIVE	COMPARATIVE	SUPERLATIVE
much	more	most
badly	worse	worst
well	better	best
far	farther	farthest
little	less	least

EXERCISE 1

Decide whether the underlined adverbs are in the positive, comparative, or superlative form and write the correct name on the line provided. The first one is done for you.

1. _____positive_____ Casey <u>foolishly</u> left her bike outside during the storm.

2. _____ The rain fell <u>harder</u> in the afternoon.

3. _____ Mike runs <u>more quickly</u> than Ted.

4. _____ Which planet is <u>nearest</u> to the sun?

5. _____ This is the <u>most tightly</u> wound coil.

6. _____ My teacher's cold is <u>worse</u> than my mother's.

7. _____ I tried to speak <u>intelligently</u> during our presentation.

8. _____ Nadeem studies <u>more carefully</u> than Ian.

9. _____ We were asked to speak <u>softly</u> in our groups.

10. _____ Rebecca lives <u>farthest</u> from the school.

EXERCISE 2

Fill in the missing adverbs in the chart below.

POSITIVE	COMPARATIVE	SUPERLATIVE
1. early	earlier	_____
2. quietly	_____	most quietly
3. _____	worse	worst
4. close	_____	closest
5. suddenly	more suddenly	_____
6. far	_____	farthest
7. _____	nearer	nearest
8. carefully	more carefully	_____
9. much	more	_____
10. creatively	_____	most creatively
11. _____	faster	fastest
12. _____	more noisily	most noisily
13. little	less	_____
14. late	_____	latest
15. _____	better	best

USING "GOOD" AND "WELL"

Some people use an adjective when they should use an adverb. Others use an adverb when they should use an adjective. *Good* is an adjective used to describe a person, place, or object/thing. It answers the question, "What kind?" Most of the time *well* is an adverb used to describe a verb. It answers the question, "How?"

Here are some examples of *good* and *well* used correctly.

Our class had a **good** time on field day.

Good is an adjective describing the noun *time*. It answers the question, "What kind of time?"

We played **well** together.

Well is an adverb describing the verb *played*. It answers the question, "How did we play?"

It's a **good** idea to know the rules of a game before you play.

Good is an adjective describing the noun *idea*. It answers the question, "What kind of idea?"

We listened **well** as our coach explained the rules.

Well is an adverb that describes the verb *listened*. It answers the question, "How did we listen?"

EXERCISE 1

Circle the correct word in parentheses in each sentence below.

1. Don't swim in deep water unless you can swim (good, well).

2. Kelly is a (good, well) in-line skater.

3. My brother's new car runs (good, well).

4. We have had (good, well) weather all week.

5. That's a (good, well) idea for a gift!

6. My father learned to cook (good, well) by watching his mother.

7. Our family had a (good, well) vacation at the beach.

8. Grandfather carves wooden animals so (good, well).

EXERCISE 2

Use *good* or *well* to complete each sentence correctly.

1. Baseball is a _____ spectator sport for a hot summer night.

2. It is especially exciting when the team plays _____.

3. I shout encouragement loudly so the players can hear me

   _____.

4. Another _____ part of the evening is eating a tasty hot dog.

5. A cold soda goes _____ with the hot dog.

6. A _____ player at first base is essential.

7. That player needs to catch _____.

8. It's a _____ feeling when our favorite team wins.

EXERCISE 3

On the lines below, write two sentences using the adjective *good* correctly.

_____

_____

_____

On the lines below, write two sentences using the adverb *well* correctly.

_____

_____

_____

THE ADVERB "NOT"

The word *not* is an adverb. It is called a **negative adverb** because it gives a negative meaning to the verbs it describes.

Here are some examples of *not* describing a verb:

Her younger sister did **not** put her toys away.
We have **not** found our missing kitten.

As in these sentences, the adverb *not* will usually be in the middle of a verb phrase.

Not can also be found in verb/adverb contractions such as *wasn't*. *Wasn't* stands for the two words *was not*.

Adele **wasn't** at her bus stop on time.
Adele **was not** at her bus stop on time.

EXERCISE 1

Rewrite the following sentences and change each sentence by adding the adverb *not* to describe the verb or verb phrase. The first one is done for you.

1. Our family will drive to California.

   Our family will not drive to California.
   _____

2. I am going to sleepaway camp this summer.

   _____

3. I have learned to diagram adverbs.

   _____

4. The Grodsteins are moving in the spring.

_____

5. Ms. Buchanan said that I could take the test next week.

_____

Now write five sentences of your own, using the adverb *not* to describe the verb phrase.

_____

_____

_____

_____

_____

SENTENCE DIAGRAMMING USING GRAPHIC ORGANIZERS

This section shows how to diagram adverbs.

The audience clapped loudly.

The simple subject is *audience*, the simple predicate is *clapped*, and the adverb *loudly* tells how the audience clapped. Here is how to diagram those three parts of the sentence:

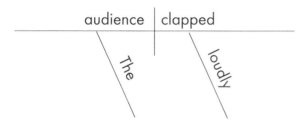

Notice how the adverb is placed on a diagonal line going from left to right under *clapped*.

Here is another example:

Yael sang happily.

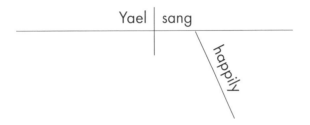

The simple subject is *Yael*; it is placed before the vertical line. The simple predicate is *sang*; it is placed after the vertical line. The adverb *happily* answers the question, "How did Yael sing?" It goes on a diagonal line under *sang*.

Look at the next sentence.

Tisha could not play with us after school.

The simple subject is *Tisha*, the simple predicate is *could play*, and *not* is the negative adverb describing the verb phrase *could play*. It is diagrammed as follows:

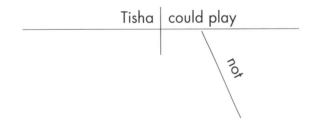

EXERCISE 1

Place the simple subjects, simple predicates, and adverbs on the correct lines in the graphic organizers below.

1. Our new neighbors unpacked immediately.

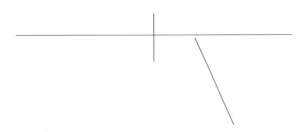

2. Our principal smiled cheerfully.

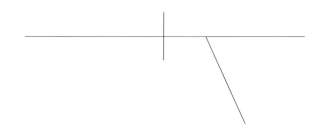

3. The chorus sang well at the concert.

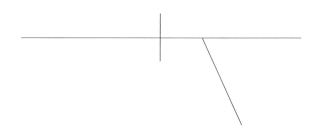

4. The guest speaker had not arrived.

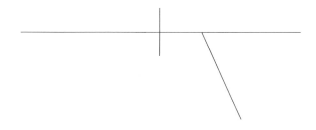

5. Our track team runs fast.

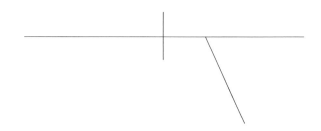

ADVERB REVIEW EXERCISES

REMEMBER: An adverb is a word that describes a verb and often answers one of these questions: "How?" "When?" "Where?" Many (but not all) adverbs end in *-ly*.

EXERCISE 1

Underline the adverbs in the following sentences.

1. Egypt, a country in Africa, can boast proudly of its heritage.

2. Egyptian families have lived contentedly along the banks of the Nile River for thousands of years.

3. They have comfortably enjoyed the warm climate of the Nile Valley.

4. Fortunately for us, artists portrayed the way Egyptians lived their lives in ancient times.

5. Whether rich or poor, the ancient Egyptians believed strongly in life after death.

6. They were clearly as proud of their daughters as they were of their sons.

7. We know from wall paintings that Egyptian families definitely played and enjoyed board games.

8. You will surely want to learn more about these fascinating people.

EXERCISE 2

One adverb is underlined in each sentence below; draw an arrow from the adverb to the verb it describes.

1. <u>Yesterday</u> we began studying maps.

2. We learned that maps and globes portray the earth <u>differently</u>.

3. Mapmakers are <u>always</u> concerned about area, direction, distance, and shape.

4. Flat maps do <u>not</u> show the round earth exactly.

5. Although globes <u>accurately</u> show sizes, locations, and distances, maps do not.

6. Some of the first maps were <u>crudely</u> painted on animal skins.

7. Polynesian islanders <u>cleverly</u> made maps out of palm leaves woven through reeds.

8. The oldest maps that exist <u>today</u> were made 4,000 years ago in the ancient civilization of Babylon.

9. When mapmakers work, they calculate their mathematics <u>carefully</u>.

10. Tomorrow we will go <u>outside</u> to make maps of the playground.

EXERCISE 3

In each sentence below, the adverb is underlined and an arrow points to the word it describes. Decide whether the adverb answers *how*, *where*, or *when*, and write *how*, *where*, or *when* on the line in front of the sentence.

1. _____ <u>Yesterday</u> our sixth graders won the county Quiz Bowl.

2. _____ Cory, the captain, <u>proudly</u> accepted the trophy.

3. _____ Students, teachers, and parents <u>enthusiastically</u> support the Quiz Bowl club.

4. _____ The team meets <u>regularly</u> with a faculty advisor.

5. _____ At first, they were <u>somewhat</u> discouraged.

6. _____ Ms. Fernandez, our principal, <u>strongly</u> encouraged them to stick with it.

7. _____ 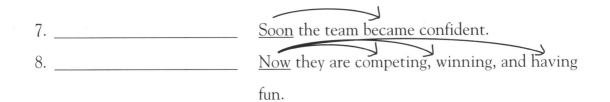 Soon the team became confident.

8. _____ Now they are competing, winning, and having

fun.

REMEMBER: Adverbs, like adjectives, can be used to make comparisons. The three forms for comparison are called positive, comparative, and superlative. Positive describes, comparative compares two things or people, and superlative compares more than two things or people.

EXERCISE 4

Decide whether the underlined adverbs are in the positive, comparative, or superlative form and write the correct name of the form on the line provided.

1. _____ Shirani and Megan skipped <u>happily</u> down

the walk.

2. _____ I run <u>farther</u> each day.

3. _____ Their project was completed <u>most creatively</u>.

4. _____ He spoke <u>softly</u> at first.

5. _____ Our team works <u>best</u>.

6. _____ I wish I could see my grandparents

<u>more frequently</u>.

7. _____ If we work too <u>fast</u>, our answers may not be

accurate.

8. _____ It rained <u>harder</u> yesterday.

EXERCISE 5

On the line next to each adverb, write the comparative form.

1. much   _____

2. close   _____

3. little   _____

4. late   _____

5. creatively   _____

Write the superlative form.

1. badly   _____

2. suddenly   _____

3. frequently   _____

4. fast   _____

5. much   _____

 REMEMBER: *Good* is an adjective used to describe a person, place, or object/thing. It answers the question, "What kind?" Most of the time *well* is an adverb used to describe a verb. It answers the question, "How?"

EXERCISE 6

Use *good* or *well* to complete each sentence correctly.

1. Aunt Louise cooked a _____ meal for the family on Sunday.

2. She always cooks _____, but this time she outdid herself.

3. The roast was a _____ size for fifteen people.

4. Aunt Louise even bakes _____.

5. Her desserts were really _____.

6. After she fed us so _____, she surprised everyone with little gifts.

7. She is such a _____ aunt.

8. All of us think _____ of her.

EXERCISE 7

Write three sentences of your own using *good* as an adjective.

_____

_____

_____

Write three sentences of your own using *well* as an adverb.

_____

_____

_____

 REMEMBER: The word *not* is an adverb. It is called a negative adverb because it gives a negative meaning to the verb it describes.

Change each of the following sentences by adding the adverb *not* to describe the verb or verb phrase. Then rewrite the sentences.

1. Megan is joining the Quiz Bowl team next year.

   _____

2. Ari will come to the playground after school.

   _____

3. The teachers are planning the exams today.

   _____

4. Our track team has entered the county meet.

   _____

5. The mayor will run for election again.

   _____

EXERCISE 9

Now write five sentences of your own using the adverb *not* to describe the verb phrase.

_____

_____

_____

_____

_____

REMEMBER: An adverb is diagrammed on a diagonal line going from left to right under the verb or verb phrase it describes.

 **EXERCISE 10**

Place the simple subjects, simple predicates, and adverbs on the correct lines in the diagrams below each sentence.

1. The skaters glided gracefully.

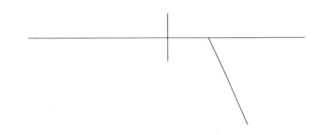

2. The sprinters ran fast.

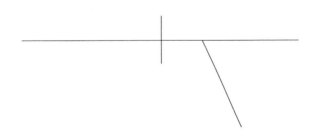

3. Lightning strikes quickly.

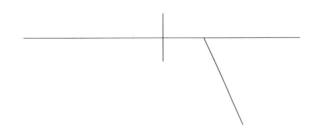

4. The three students read happily.

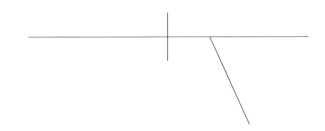

5. Aziza solved the problem immediately.

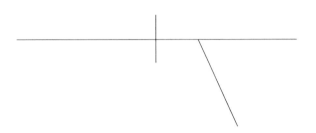

ABOUT EXPANDING SENTENCES

You have learned that a sentence is a group of words that expresses a complete thought; it contains a subject (the *who* or *what*) and a verb/verb phrase (the action word or linking word).

This chapter will take you beyond the subject/verb construction. It will show you ways to express yourself with fuller sentences using greater detail. You will learn about combining subjects, combining predicates, combining related sentences, and adding prepositional and noun phrases to create longer, more interesting sentences.

COMBINING SUBJECTS

Sometimes two subjects can be combined. When the predicate is the same but the subjects are different, you can form a **compound subject** with the conjunction *and*. (A **conjunction** is a word that joins similar parts of a sentence. Three common ones are *and*, *but*, and *or*.) Longer sentences are often more interesting to the reader than short, choppy ones.

Look at the example below:

Javier studied for several hours.

The complete subject is *Javier*; the complete predicate is *studied for several hours*.

Mike studied for several hours.

The complete subject is *Mike*; the complete predicate is the same as in the sentence above.

You can combine the subjects (*Javier and Mike*) and use the same predicate to have one sentence with a **compound subject.**

Javier and Mike studied for several hours.

Here is another example:

The midfielders had played hard.
The backfielders had played hard.

Above are two sentences with different subjects but the same predicate. Combine the subjects (*The midfielders and backfielders*) and use the same predicate to create one sentence with a **compound subject.**

The midfielders and backfielders had played hard.

Here is one more example:

The pizzas at Ari's party were great.
The videos at Ari's party were great.

These two sentences can be combined to form one sentence with a **compound subject.**

The pizzas and videos at Ari's party were great.

EXERCISE 1

Combine the subjects in the pairs of sentences below using the conjunction *and* to form single sentences with compound subjects. The first one is done for you.

1. The president spoke about the importance of education.

   The vice president spoke about the importance of education.

   The president and the vice president spoke about the importance of education.

2. Beverly Cleary won several children's book awards.

   Gary Paulsen won several children's book awards.

   _____

3. Tornadoes are fierce spiraling storms.

   Cyclones are fierce spiraling storms.

   _____

4. Warm currents affect weather and climate.

   Wind patterns affect weather and climate.

   _____

5. Diamonds are valuable gemstones.

   Emeralds are valuable gemstones.

   _____

6. My brother loves working on cars.

   My sister loves working on cars.

   _____

EXERCISE 2

Write five sentences of your own using compound subjects.

_____

_____

_____

_____

_____

COMBINING PREDICATES

Sometimes two sentences can be combined when the subjects are the same but the predicates are different. You can form a **compound predicate** by using the conjunction *and* to combine the two predicates.

Look at the example below:

Samantha plays the recorder.

The complete subject is *Samantha*; the complete predicate is *plays the recorder*.

Samantha takes gymnastics lessons.

The complete subject is *Samantha*; the complete predicate is *takes gymnastics lessons*.

You can create one sentence by combining the predicates because the subject is the same. The conjunction *and* is used to form a compound predicate.

Samantha plays the recorder and takes gymnastics lessons.

Here is another example:

Last night Colin wrote a book report.
Last night Colin studied the new spelling words.

The subject is the same, so the two predicates can be combined using the conjunction *and* to form a compound predicate.

Last night Colin wrote a book report and studied the new spelling words.

Here is one more example:

The police presented an assembly on bike safety.
The police spoke to the students about bike registration.

The subject is the same, so the two predicates can be combined using *and* to form a compound predicate.

The police presented an assembly on bike safety and spoke to the students about bike registration.

EXERCISE 1

Combine the predicates in the pairs of sentences below to form single sentences with compound predicates joined by the conjunction *and*. The first one is done for you.

1. Sojourner Truth wanted to abolish slavery.

   Sojourner Truth thought women should have the right to vote.

   Sojourner Truth wanted to abolish slavery and thought women should have

   the right to vote.

2. Photographs provide memories.

   Photographs help preserve history.

   _____

3. Dancers and athletes practice long hours.

   Dancers and athletes keep fit.

   _____

4. The National Museum of American Art was founded in 1829.

   The National Museum of American Art now has the largest collection of

   American art in the world.

   _____

   _____

5. Our Constitution guarantees freedom.

   Our Constitution provides justice for all.

   _____

6. The wind rustled the sails.

   The wind made the boat glide over the waves.

   _____

EXERCISE 2

Write five sentences of your own using compound predicates.

_____

_____

_____

_____

_____

COMBINING SENTENCES WITH CONJUNCTIONS

You can make sentences more interesting by varying their lengths. When two short sentences have related ideas, you can combine them. The new sentence is called a **compound sentence.**

Here are some examples:

Carly's mother is a reporter.
Her father is a store owner.
Carly's mother is a reporter, **and** her father is a store owner.

The sky was dark all day.
It didn't rain.
The sky was dark all day, **but** it didn't rain.

Should we try other reference books?
Should we change our topic?
Should we try other reference books, **or** should we change our topic?

I wanted to get a good grade.
I studied very hard.
I wanted to get a good grade, **so** I studied very hard.

Notice that when each pair of sentences was combined, a **comma** (,) and a **conjunction** were used to make the connection. A **conjunction** connects words or groups of words. The four conjunctions used in the sentences above were _and_, _but_, _or_, and _so_. Learn these four conjunctions.

EXERCISE 1

Use the conjunction given to combine each pair of related sentences to make a compound sentence. Don't forget to place a comma *before* the conjunction.

1. or   We can skate to the park. We can ride our bikes.

   _____

2. but   The boys chose to skate. The girls rode their bikes.

   _____

3. so   The boys were not ready. The girls left.

   _____

4. and   Ted took the lead. Mike rode second.

   _____

5. but   They wanted to play soccer. The field had just been seeded.

   _____

6. and   A sign was posted. The field was roped off.

   _____

7. so   Geoff had brought a basketball. They decided to shoot baskets.

   _____

8. or   They could practice shots. They could play actual games.

   _____

9. and   They decided to practice first. Then they would pick teams and play.

   _____

10. but One team won all the games. Everyone had a good time.

   _____

EXERCISE 2

Below are ten compound sentences. Underline the two short sentences that were combined to make each compound sentence. Do not underline the commas and the conjunctions.

1. Elizabeth Blackwell was a British American, and she was the first woman to receive a medical degree in the United States.

2. Elizabeth was born near Bristol, England, but her family moved to New York City when she was eleven.

3. From there the family moved to Jersey City, New Jersey, and they later moved to Cincinnati, Ohio.

4. Her father died, so her mother, her sisters, and she went to work.

5. Elizabeth accepted a job as a teacher, but she had other dreams.

6. She wanted to be a doctor, but she had difficulty being accepted at a medical school.

7. She had hoped to go to Harvard, but she was accepted at Geneva College.

8. A serious infection left her blind in one eye, so she ended her plans to be a surgeon.

9. She could practice general medicine, or she could leave the profession.

10. She opened a hospital for women and children, and she established the Women's Medical College.

ADDING PHRASES TO EXPAND SENTENCES

Sentences should create images in the mind of the reader. They can do this by providing details and specific information. Writers can provide details and specifics by adding phrases to their sentences.

REMEMBER: An appositive is a word or words with the same meaning as a nearby noun or proper noun. It is another way of identifying that noun.

Look at the sentence below:

My geography project is about **Aruba.**

Look at that same sentence with an appositive phrase added to it:

My geography project is about Aruba, **a small tropical island.**

The second sentence provides a clearer picture for the reader.
You can create an even clearer picture by adding one or more prepositional phrases to the appositive:

My geography project is about Aruba, a small tropical island **off the coast of Venezuela.**

Off the coast of Venezuela is a combination of two prepositional phrases: *off the coast* and *of Venezuela.*

REMEMBER: A prepositional phrase is made up of a preposition, its object, and any word or words that describe that object. The preposition shows a relationship between its object and some other word in the sentence. Look again at Chapter 6 if you need a review of prepositions.

In the phrase *off the coast, off* is the preposition; *coast* is its object. The phrase describes the noun *island.*

In the phrase *of Venezuela, of* is the preposition; *Venezuela* is its object. The phrase tells which coast.

Here is another example of how to lengthen and strengthen a sentence:

The tree swayed.
The tree, a young willow, swayed in the evening breeze.

An appositive and a prepositional phrase were added to give a clearer picture. The appositive *a young willow* tells what type of tree; the prepositional phrase *in the evening breeze* tells when and how it swayed.

Sentences can always be made more vivid by adding adjectives and adverbs.

The young willow tree swayed gently in the evening breeze.

This time the adjectives *young* and *willow* were added before the noun *tree*. The adverb *gently* was added to describe how the tree swayed.

Now add some words of your own to lengthen and strengthen *The tree swayed*. Rewrite the sentence below.

_____

_____

EXERCISE 1

Expand the following sentences by adding appositives, prepositional phrases, adjectives, and adverbs. The first one is done for you.

1. The man smiled.

   The cheerful man in the straw hat smiled happily at his grandchildren.

2. Ethan ran.

   _____

3. The cars sped.

   _____

4. The waves roared.

   _____

5. The moon glowed.

   _____

6. The students practiced.

   _____

Write whether the underlined word or words are adjectives, adverbs, appositives, or prepositional phrases.

1. _____ Some state capitals have <u>interesting</u> backgrounds.

2. _____ The former capital of Pennsylvania, <u>Philadelphia</u>, has been its leading city for three centuries.

3. _____ Richmond, Virginia's capital, was the capital of the Confederacy <u>during the Civil War</u>.

4. _____ San Antonio was the capital <u>of Texas</u> when it was a territory.

5. _____ Knoxville was the capital <u>of Tennessee</u> before Nashville.

6. _____ Nashville, Tennessee, is a <u>major</u> music recording center.

7. _____ Savannah, Georgia, <u>quaintly</u> offers its southern hospitality to thousands of tourists each year.

8. _____ It was the capital of Georgia before the current capital, <u>Atlanta</u>.

9. _____ Montpelier, the capital of Vermont, has <u>approximately</u> 8,300 residents.

10. _____ It has the distinction of being the capital <u>with the fewest residents</u>.

SENTENCE DIAGRAMMING USING GRAPHIC ORGANIZERS

This section will review how to diagram adjectives, adverbs, appositives, and prepositional phrases. It will also show how to diagram compound subjects, compound predicates, and compound sentences.

Adjectives are written on a diagonal line under the noun they describe. The line goes from left to right.

All teachers plan.

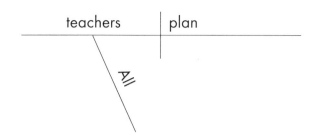

Adverbs are written on a diagonal line under the verb they describe. The line goes from left to right.

All teachers plan carefully.

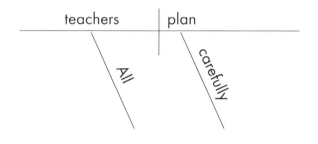

Appositives are written in parentheses on the line immediately after the noun they describe.

My teacher, Ms. Buchanan, plans carefully.

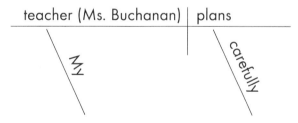

Prepositional phrases are diagrammed under the word they describe. The preposition is written on a diagonal. The object goes on a line that extends to the right from the end of the diagonal. Any adjectives in front of the object are written on a diagonal under the noun they describe.

My teacher, Ms. Buchanan, plans carefully during her lunch period.

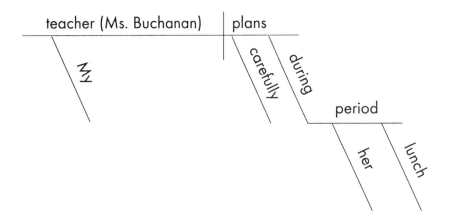

Compound subjects, compound predicates, and compound sentences are diagrammed in a slightly different way.

Compound subjects are diagrammed like this:

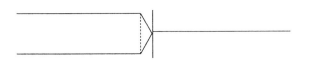

The subjects are written on the short horizontal lines and the word *and* is written on the dotted vertical line.

Mike and Ari played.

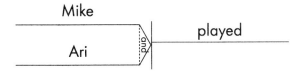

Tisha and Karim sang in the chorus.

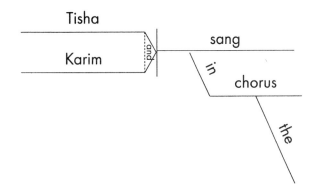

Compound predicates are diagrammed similarly, but the organizer faces the opposite way.

The girls joked and laughed.

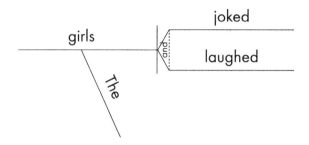

Mike played in the park and then studied.

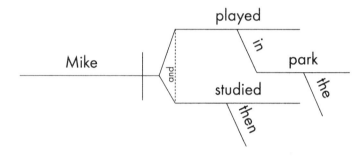

Compound sentences are diagrammed as two separate sentences. They are connected by the conjunction on a line that looks like steps. Look at the compound sentence below:

Scott biked to school, but his brother walked.

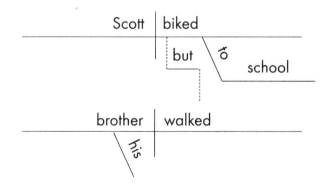

Notice that the stepped line for the conjunction goes from the verb in the first sentence to the verb in the second. It is a good idea to diagram each sentence first; then write in the conjunction.

Here is another example:

The Weather Channel predicted rain, so I took an umbrella.

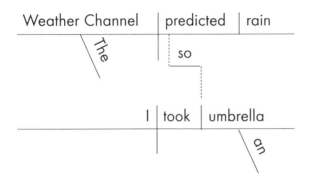

EXERCISE 1

On the graphic organizers provided, diagram all of the words in the following sentences.

1. Lorraine Hansberry wrote a famous play, *A Raisin in the Sun*.

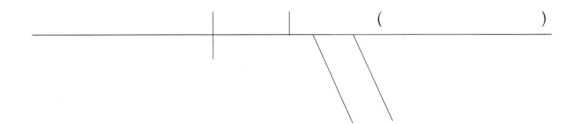

2. The play is noted for its challenging themes.

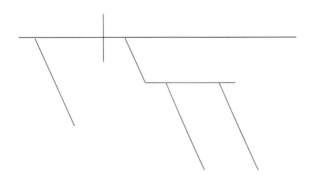

3. It shows an important time in the life of one black family.

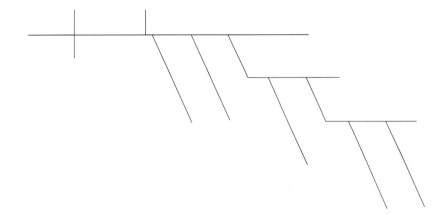

4. A conflict threatens the family relationships.

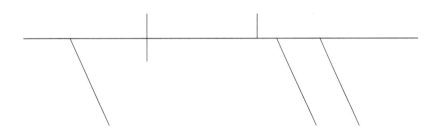

5. *A Raisin in the Sun* was made into a powerful movie.

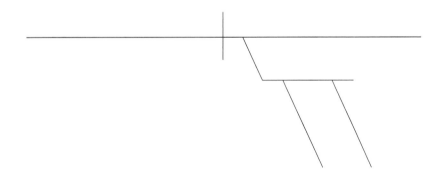

6. The title of the play quotes a poem, *A Dream Deferred.*

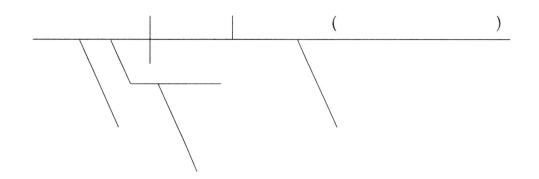

7. Langston Hughes, author of *A Dream Deferred,* and Lorraine Hansberry were two talented people.

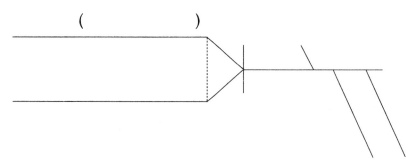

8. Langston Hughes wrote poetry and translated Spanish poems.

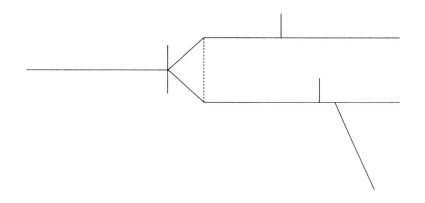

EXPANDING SENTENCES REVIEW EXERCISES

 REMEMBER: When the predicates are the same, you can combine the subjects with the conjunction *and* to form one sentence with a compound subject.

 EXERCISE 1

Combine the subjects in the pairs of sentences below using the conjunction *and* to form single sentences with compound subjects.

1. More species of plants flourish in tropical rain forests than in any other type of region.

   More species of animals flourish in tropical rain forests than in any other type of region.

   _____

   _____

2. Tropical rain forests can exist on high mountains.

   Icy glaciers can exist on high mountains.

   _____

3. Wind can carve rocks into unusual shapes.

   Rain can carve rocks into unusual shapes.

   _____

4. Moving water can provide clean energy.

   Wind can provide clean energy.

   _____

5. Squids swim by squirting out water that propels them backwards.

Octopuses swim by squirting out water that propels them backwards.

_____

_____

6. Turtles are long-distance travelers.

Salmon are long-distance travelers.

_____

7. Javan rhinos are close to extinction.

South China tigers are close to extinction.

_____

8. Earthquakes are among the most serious natural disasters.

Volcanic eruptions are among the most serious natural disasters.

_____

_____

 REMEMBER: When the subjects are the same, you can combine the predicates to form one sentence with a compound predicate.

EXERCISE 2

Combine the predicates in the pairs of sentences below to form single sentences with compound predicates.

1. Water warms more slowly than land.

Water cools more slowly than land.

_____

2. Volcanic activity may take place on land.

   Volcanic activity may occur under the sea.

   _____

3. Australia has turned around from its original position.

   Australia has been moving slowly northward.

   _____

4. Fossil fuels are made from the remains of plants and animals.

   Fossil fuels formed slowly over millions of years.

   _____

5. Classification groups living things by similarities.

   Classification shows how one group is related to another.

   _____

6. Feathers keep a bird warm.

   Feathers help make flying possible.

   _____

7. The sun lies at the center of our solar system.

   The sun has been like a power station for Earth.

   _____

8. Light travels in a wave.

   Light moves faster than anything else.

   _____

REMEMBER: Compound sentences are formed by connecting two related sentences with a comma and a conjunction.

EXERCISE 3

Combine each pair of related sentences with a comma and a conjunction. Then write five compound sentences of your own. Four common conjunctions are *and, but, or,* and *so.*

1. The primary colors are yellow, blue, and red. All three added together make brown.

   _____

2. Light travels very quickly. Sound travels more slowly.

   _____

3. Light from a flashlight spreads out. Laser light hardly spreads at all.

   _____

4. Sunlight sometimes makes our eyes blink and water. Without it we could not see.

   _____

Write your own compound sentences on the lines below.

1. _____
2. _____
3. _____
4. _____
5. _____

REMEMBER: You can add details to your sentences using adjectives, adverbs, appositives, and prepositional phrases.

EXERCISE 4

Add adjectives, adverbs, appositives, or prepositional phrases to the sentences below to make them more interesting. You may add more than one type of detail to each sentence.

1. The audience clapped.

_____

2. Astronauts prepared.

_____

3. The woman jumped.

_____

4. The animals were startled.

_____

5. The experiment failed.

_____

6. The flowers blossomed.

_____

7. The Patels ate dinner.

_____

8. The teacher showed a video.

_____

9. The students made projects.

_____

10. Josiah read.

_____

REMEMBER: Graphic organizers use specific lines for specific sentence parts.

EXERCISE 5

Write the sentence parts in the correct places on the graphic organizers provided.

1. Alex, my brother, plays in a band.

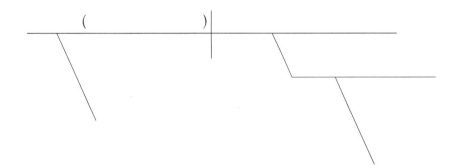

2. The audience laughed heartily.

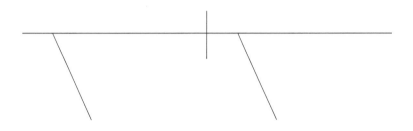

3. Our youth group participated in a fund-raiser.

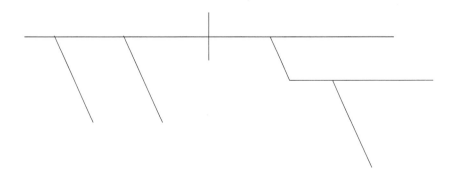

4. Harry and his sister, Morgen, drove to her college.

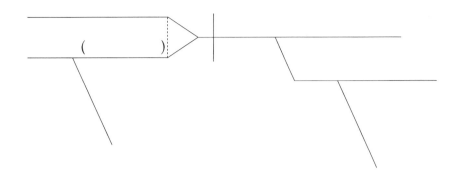

5. The school of fish swam into an underwater cave.

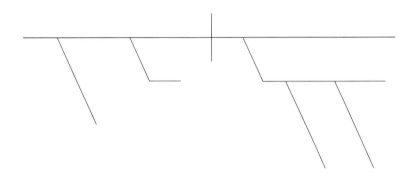

6. Carly and her sister played in the family room.

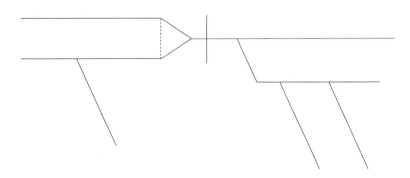

7. Noel wrote to his grandmother and talked on the phone.

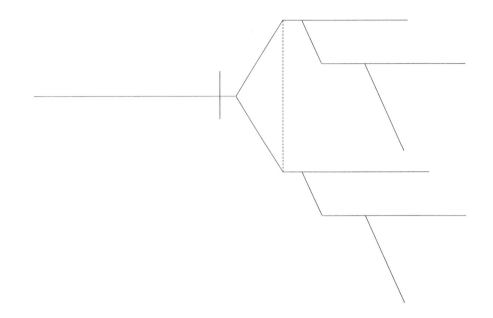

8. Dad cooked dinner, and I washed the dishes.

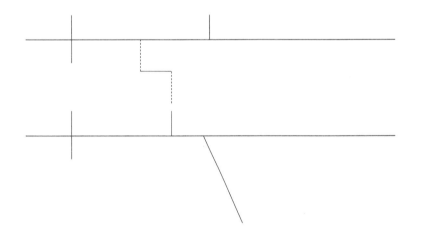

FINAL REVIEW EXERCISES

Before you begin these exercises you may want to go back and review the lessons. You may look back to review any lessons and rules that you cannot remember when doing these pages.

EXERCISE 1

In the sentences below underline the complete subject once. Underline the complete predicate twice. Draw a vertical line (|) between the subject and predicate.

1. Mr. Williams decorated a new bulletin board in the school hallway.

2. Students' family members sent in photographs and sketches.

3. The informal pictures showed the families reading together.

4. Some family pets were included, too!

5. People like relaxing and being comfortable while they read.

6. Every student wrote about what was in the pictures.

7. They told about favorite books read at home.

8. Some artistic volunteers drew a border of books around the edges of the board.

9. Many people praised the students' interesting work.

10. Other teachers and students asked if they could make a similar presentation.

11. Mr. Williams and his students were proud to have started a trend.

12. Christa McAuliffe School is a community of readers.

EXERCISE 2

In the following sentences underline the simple subject once and underline the simple predicate twice.

1. Frogs belong to a group of creatures that are cold-blooded.

2. They live both in water and on land.

3. Amphibians such as frogs often lay eggs in water.

4. Eggs float on top of the water in a jellylike substance.

5. Soon they hatch into tadpoles.

6. The young tadpoles look more like fish than frogs.

7. Most types lose their gills and tails in about two or three months.

8. Legs and lungs develop next.

9. Most frogs grow teeth.

10. It can take about a year for a frog to complete its development.

EXERCISE 3

Read the groups of words below. Write the word *sentence* on the line if the words form a complete thought. Write the word *fragment* on the line if the words do not form a complete thought. On the diagram below each group of words write the simple subject and simple predicate. If the sentence is missing one or both, create your own. The first one is done for you.

1. <u>fragment</u>   The tourists' cameras hang around their necks.

cameras | hang

2. _____ The baby smiled at the colorful mobile.

_____|_____
                |

3. _____ Delicious chocolate milk in the glass.

_____|_____
                |

4. _____ Sings in the school chorus every year.

_____|_____
                |

5. _____ I run fast.

_____|_____
                |

6. _____ In the summer the most fun thing.

_____|_____
                |

7. _____ John loves imaginative stories.

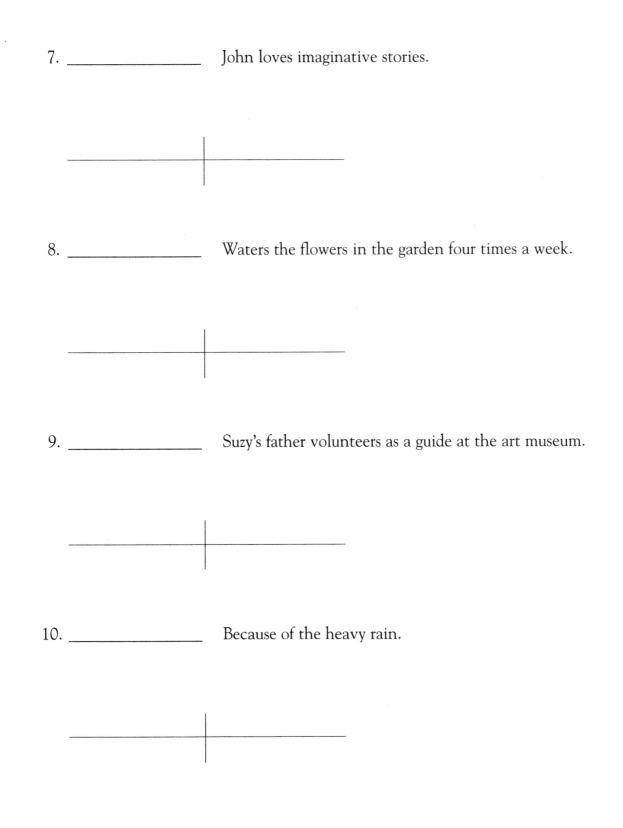

8. _____ Waters the flowers in the garden four times a week.

9. _____ Suzy's father volunteers as a guide at the art museum.

10. _____ Because of the heavy rain.

EXERCISE 4

Identify each sentence by filling in the line with the appropriate word: *declarative, interrogative, imperative command, imperative request,* or *exclamatory*. Place the proper punctuation after each sentence.

1. _____ What month were you born

2. _____ My mother said I was born on the hottest day of the summer

3. _____ In my family it is a tradition to name a baby after a grandparent

4. _____ Please tell me how your parents chose your name

5. _____ That's funny

6. _____ Write down how you spell it

7. _____ My sister, Emily, is named for my father's mother

8. _____ Can you imagine how it would feel to have a namesake

9. _____ If I ever have a son, I will name him for my father

10. _____ Having triplets would be a lot of work

EXERCISE 5

Write a sentence of your own that fits each type named. Be sure to punctuate it properly.

1. Interrogative _____

2. Declarative _____

3. Exclamatory _____

4. Imperative _____

EXERCISE 6

Place the simple subjects and the simple predicates in the diagrams provided.

1. The large picture looks tilted.

2. The old light bulb burned out.

3. I need a higher desk.

4. My dog ate my homework!

5. That story is hard to believe!

Underline the verb or verb phrase in each sentence. On the line after each sentence, write whether it is an action or a linking verb.

1. A suspended magnet will point approximately to the north. _____

2. This led to the creation of the compass. _____

3. Every magnet has two definite poles. _____

4. These poles are opposite in nature. _____

5. Unlike poles attract each other. _____

6. Oersted, a Danish scientist, discovered in 1820 that a wire carrying an electric current also created a magnetic field. _____

7. After that, scientists created the powerful electromagnet. _____

8. The telephone, electric lights, and the radio were invented later. _____

9. These were important and useful discoveries! _____

Fill in the chart below with the simple subjects, the helping verbs, and the main verbs from the following sentences.

1. Young whales are called calves.

2. A baby whale is fed on its mother's milk.

3. These water mammals have descended from ancestors that lived on land.

4. They did adapt for life in the water.

5. Certain changes had taken place in their bodies over millions of years.

6. These sea creatures can breathe through their lungs.

7. Blowholes must make it easier to breathe at the surface of the water.

8. Under water these nostrils will close by little valves.

9. Whales may rise to the water's surface every five or ten minutes.

10. Here they will exhale old air and water vapor.

SUBJECT   HELPING VERB   MAIN VERB

_____   _____   _____

_____   _____   _____

_____   _____   _____

_____   _____   _____

_____   _____   _____

_____   _____   _____

_____   _____   _____

_____   _____   _____

_____   _____   _____

EXERCISE 9

Circle the correct singular or plural subject or verb in the following sentences.

1. Sometimes our teacher (pass, passes) along bits of old-fashioned advice.

2. Mr. Williams (call, calls) them "pearls of wisdom," but he has to explain some of them.

3. Birds of a feather (flock, flocks) together.

4. A watched (pot, pots) never boils.

5. A stitch in time (save, saves) nine.

6. Neither a (borrower, borrowers) nor a lender be.

7. A (picture, pictures) is worth a thousand words.

8. A bird in the hand (are, is) worth two in the bush.

9. A dog's (bark, barks) may be worse than his bite.

10. If you can't (says, say) something nice, don't say anything at all.

EXERCISE 10

Underline each action verb and identify its tense. Then write *present, past,* or *future* on the line next to it.

1. _____ A nightingale sings sweetly.

2. _____ My parents and I watched a movie last night.

3. _____ I will stay home tomorrow if I still feel sick.

4. _____ Dolphins breathe air through a nostril on the top of the head.

5. _____ We saw a school of fish at the lake.

6. _____ Our teacher will not assign homework on the weekend.

7. _____ He gives us a test every Friday.

8. _____ My brother saves part of his allowance every week.

9. _____ He learned about saving from our parents.

10. _____ I will learn about wise planning too.

EXERCISE 11

Write two sentences in the present tense.

_____

_____

Write two sentences in the past tense.

_____

_____

Write two sentences in the future tense.

_____

_____

Change the verb in the first column to the past tense and write it in the sentence.

1. create   Jake and Adele _____ a neighborhood newspaper.

2. dance   Megan _____ in the recital with her two sisters.

3. mark   Ms. Buchanan _____ the test papers at lunchtime.

4. compute   Several students _____ the problems in their heads.

5. skate   We _____ until dusk.

6. kick   Geoff _____ the soccer ball into the goalpost.

7. trot   The horse _____ around the corral.

8. participate   Everyone in our class _____ in the talent show.

Use the form of the verb in italics to complete the following sentences. Write the correct form on the line.

1. past participle of *dream*

   Arjun has _____ of a trip to India.

2. present of *imagine*

   I _____ a future as a doctor.

3. present participle of *clap*

   The audience was _____ for a long time.

4. past of *admire*

   Javier _____ the way Mike dribbled a soccer ball.

5. past participle of *stop*

The teacher has _____ giving tests on Monday morning.

6. present of *act*

Rachel _____ in every school play.

EXERCISE 14

Complete the chart below by writing in the present participle, the past, and the past participle of the present tense verbs shown in column 1.

	PRESENT PARTICIPLE	PAST	PAST PARTICIPLE
1. break	_____	_____	have, has, had _____
2. choose	_____	_____	have, has, had _____
3. come	_____	_____	have, has, had _____
4. give	_____	_____	have, has, had _____
5. keep	_____	_____	have, has, had _____
6. say	_____	_____	have, has, had _____
7. see	_____	_____	have, has, had _____
8. take	_____	_____	have, has, had _____
9. tell	_____	_____	have, has, had _____
10. wring	_____	_____	have, has, had _____

Write a diamonte poem in the past tense. Use the form shown in Chapter 3 (Verbs). The poem's shape will look like a diamond. The first line has two words, the second line has four words, the third line has six words, the fourth line has eight words, the fifth line has six words, the sixth line has four words, and the last line has two words.

_____

_____

_____

_____

_____

_____

EXERCISE 16

In the sentences below, some words are underlined. Write the contraction for these words on the line in front of each sentence.

1. _____ We could not imagine why he was so late!

2. _____ She had not locked the front door.

3. _____ You should not arrive too early.

4. _____ Sometimes the custodian has not unlocked the doors.

5. _____ I will not be able to go to practice today.

6. _____ Mr. Fischetti had not yet picked the captain and cocaptain of the team.

7. _____ Eduardo does not live far from school.

8. _____ They were not on time, which is why they missed the announcement.

EXERCISE 17

Write a paragraph telling about one of your favorite books. Be sure all of the verbs are in the present tense.

_____

_____

_____

_____

_____

_____

_____

_____

_____

_____

_____

EXERCISE 18

For the first two sentences write the simple subjects and the simple predicates in the correct places on the graphic organizers. Then make the graphic organizers for the last three sentences and write in the simple subjects and the simple predicates.

1. Everyone participated.

```
_____|_____
                  |
```

2. Lori skated.

_____

3. The team ran onto the field.

4. Jill spoke.

5. Tyler laughed out loud.

EXERCISE 19

In the sentences below, underline the nouns that name people. Circle the nouns that name places.

1. Crew members on piloted spacecrafts are called astronauts.

2. Astronauts can include scientists, engineers, medical doctors, and educators, as well as pilots.

3. U.S. spaceflights are launched from Cape Canaveral, Florida.

4. Scientists have been researching how to colonize Mars.

In these sentences, underline the nouns that name objects/things. Circle the nouns that name ideas. Double underline the nouns that name feelings.

5. A single mission can cost millions of dollars.

6. Scientists are increasing their knowledge about life in outer space.

7. Survival in space is the most important issue.

8. Can you imagine the excitement of lift-off?

9. Astronauts must feel relief when the craft reenters Earth's atmosphere.

EXERCISE 20

Write a letter to an imaginary space agency convincing them that you should be the first student to be included on a space journey. Be sure to state your qualifications and your reasons. Underline all of the nouns in your letter.

Write the underlined nouns in the following paragraphs under the correct headings in the chart below. Use each noun only once. You do not need to write on every line.

The Inuit <u>people</u> have been living in <u>Canada</u> for over 4,000 <u>years</u>. They developed a <u>culture</u> that helped them survive in the harsh arctic <u>climate</u>. Many <u>Inuit</u> built <u>igloos</u>, which they heated with whale <u>oil</u>. Native <u>animals</u> were important to the Inuit, who fished and hunted to feed their <u>families</u>. Starting in the 1960s, the <u>government</u> offered different <u>housing</u>, <u>food</u>, <u>medicine</u>, and <u>education</u> to try to help the Inuit adapt to modern life. Instead of making life easier for the Inuit, the changes caused much <u>sadness</u> and <u>confusion</u>. <u>Students</u> learning English began to forget how to speak Inuktitut, their native <u>language</u>, which meant they were unable to talk with their families. <u>Unemployment</u> was common, and traditional <u>jobs</u> such as hunting were no longer considered as important.

For many years the Inuit wanted to have their own <u>place</u> in Canada where they could protect their traditional <u>customs</u> and <u>lifestyle</u>. In 1999, after fifteen years of <u>talks</u> with the government, Canada created a new <u>territory</u> called <u>Nunavut</u>, meaning "our <u>land</u>" in Inuktitut. There were many <u>celebrations</u> for the new land. Such celebrations often included traditional Inuit food, singing, and dancing. <u>Paul Okalik</u>, Nunavut's first <u>leader</u>, helped bring new <u>business</u> and <u>technology</u> to the Inuit culture while helping to save their ancient <u>traditions</u>.

PEOPLE	PLACES	OBJECTS/ THINGS	IDEAS	FEELINGS
_____	_____	_____	_____	_____
_____	_____	_____	_____	_____
_____	_____	_____	_____	_____
_____	_____	_____	_____	_____
_____	_____	_____	_____	_____
_____	_____	_____	_____	_____
_____	_____	_____	_____	_____

PEOPLE	PLACES	OBJECTS/ THINGS	IDEAS	FEELINGS
————	————	————	————	————
————	————	————	————	————
————	————	————	————	————
————	————	————	————	————
————	————	————	————	————
————	————	————	————	————
————	————	————	————	————
————	————	————	————	————
————	————	————	————	————

EXERCISE 22

In the sentences below, underline the common nouns and circle the proper nouns.

1. Stars look like twinkling white lights in the sky.

2. The brightest star appears to be Sirius.

3. A star's color depends on its temperature.

4. Blue-white stars have the highest temperature.

5. The sun is a medium-sized star.

6. Our sun and the stars we can see from Earth are part of the Milky Way galaxy.

7. The nearest star other than our sun is named Proxima Centauri.

8. In the Northern Hemisphere constellations or groups of stars are often named after characters in myths.

9. You can find Orion by looking for the three stars that form his belt.

10. The Big Dipper is part of a constellation called Ursa Major.

11. It is one of the easiest constellations to locate.

12. Two stars in the bowl of the Big Dipper point to the North Star, located in the Little Dipper.

Rewrite each sentence and make the underlined words show the plural form.

1. Our grandmother gave us chocolate <u>candy</u>.

   _____

2. In olden days, farmers used their <u>ox</u> to pull heavy loads.

   _____

3. The <u>loaf</u> of bread had been baked in a special oven.

   _____

4. The <u>student</u> sent a thank-you letter to the guest speaker.

   _____

5. The <u>gas</u> from cars can be dangerous.

   _____

6. The <u>hill</u> and the <u>valley</u> were a beautiful sight from the airplane.

   _____

7. The books were packed away in the <u>box</u>.

   _____

8. The <u>mouse</u> had taken the cheese.

   _____

EXERCISE 24

On the lines provided, write the plurals of the nouns in the list below.

1. witch _____

2. grass _____

3. flower _____

4. man _____

5. scarf _____

6. monkey _____

7. pantry _____

8. foot _____

9. computer _____

10. lady _____

EXERCISE 25

Rewrite each noun phrase so that the underlined noun shows possession (ownership) of the other noun.

1. the pets of <u>Michael</u> _____

2. the toys of the <u>children</u> _____

3. the lids of the <u>jars</u> _____

4. the dribbling skills of <u>Ted</u> _____

5. the coin collection of my <u>grandfather</u> _____

6. the parks of the <u>cities</u> _____

7. the favorite teacher of the <u>students</u> _____

8. the color of the <u>sky</u> _____

9. the president of the <u>company</u> _____

10. the festivities of the <u>holiday</u> _____

In each of the following sentences, the appositive or appositive phrase is underlined. Draw an arrow to the noun that it refers to.

1. Dr. Abed, <u>our dentist</u>, lives on the next block.

2. The soccer coach, <u>Andy Ravitz</u>, received an award for his coaching.

3. Madeleine L'Engle has received at least one Newbery Medal, <u>a special prize for children's books</u>.

4. Earth, <u>a planet in the Milky Way</u>, is the third "rock" from the sun.

5. James Naismith, <u>the inventor of basketball</u>, cleverly combined the North American Indian game of lacrosse and the British game of soccer.

6. *Smog* is a "portmanteau word," <u>a combination of two words with some letters of each missing</u>.

7. Geoff, <u>Kyle's best friend</u>, is moving at the end of the year.

8. The coral snake, <u>a member of the cobra family</u>, lives only in the southern part of the U.S.

9. Dry ice, <u>a substance made from liquid carbon dioxide</u>, is used in the shipment of perishable foods and medicines.

10. Ms. Sylvia Fernandez, <u>our principal</u>, was born in Madrid, Spain.

EXERCISE 27

Write the nouns from each sentence in the correct places on the graphic organizers. The rest of the diagram has been done for you.

1. Carly's dad invented a special hanger for pants.

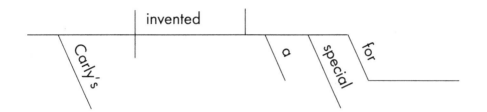

2. The girls and boys paraded in their costumes.

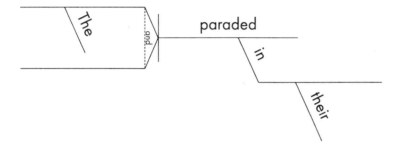

3. Kara O'Meara, my cousin from Ireland, is arriving on Saturday.

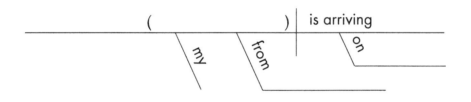

4. It is Dave's bike.

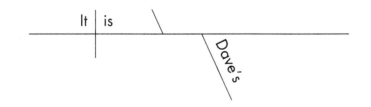

5. Megan bought several books at the book fair.

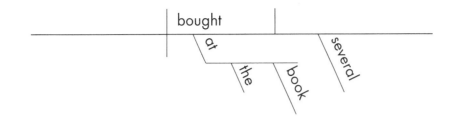

EXERCISE 28

Replace each underlined noun or noun phrase in the following sentences with the correct pronoun. Then rewrite the sentence on the line.

1. <u>Lori</u> bought <u>a baseball cap</u> with her favorite team's logo.

_____

2. <u>Geoff and his brother</u> went to visit their new cousin.

_____

3. <u>Adam</u> saw <u>a new movie</u> over the weekend.

_____

4. <u>You and I</u> make a good team!

_____

5. Please give <u>your mother and me</u> your full attention.

_____

6. Benjamin, did <u>Benjamin</u> see the video I left on the shelf?

_____

7. Mr. Williams asked <u>Rebecca and me</u> to return our overdue library books.

_____

8. Rebecca's books were heavy, so I helped <u>Rebecca</u> carry some of <u>her books</u>.

_____

EXERCISE 29

Read each pair of sentences carefully and notice the underlined pronouns in the second sentences. Find each pronoun's antecedent in the first sentences and label it by writing an A on top of that noun or pronoun.

1. The artist set up an easel in front of a painting in the museum. <u>She</u> used the same colors as Van Gogh for her drawing.

2. The movies were rated G. <u>They</u> were all appropriate for my friends and me.

3. The teacher had overloaded his bookshelf. <u>He</u> was upset when <u>it</u> collapsed.

4. The movie star waved to her fans. <u>She</u> signed several autographs.

5. The sky is a deep shade of blue. <u>It</u> has cleared after the storm.

6. My teammates and I were hoping for a time-out. <u>We</u> wanted to speak to the coach.

7. Sean was going to a special dinner. <u>His</u> grandfather was receiving an award.

8. The students were disappointed. <u>Their</u> field trip was canceled because of the rain.

EXERCISE 30

Write an S over the underlined subject pronouns and an O over the underlined object pronouns in the sentences below.

1. <u>She</u> wanted to tell <u>me</u> a secret.

2. My friends and <u>I</u> played with <u>them</u> until dinnertime.

3. Your favorite color may tell something about <u>you</u>.

4. <u>He</u> and the team captain called a practice for tomorrow.

5. My brother and sister are very excited because <u>they</u> are going to sleepaway camp.

6. <u>We</u> receive e-mail from our pen pals about once a week.

7. My grandmother called <u>us</u> from Hong Kong.

8. <u>I</u> invited <u>him</u> to eat lunch with <u>me</u>.

9. <u>We</u> told <u>her</u> to meet <u>us</u> at the park.

10. <u>It</u> is great fun to do experiments in science.

EXERCISE 31

Circle the words that correctly complete each sentence.

1. Kerri and (me, I) spent a day shopping with our cousins.

2. (I, Me) hope to go to college some day.

3. My brother, sister, and (me, I) visited our uncle's farm this weekend.

4. Tell (I, me) what you dreamed about.

5. (I and my friend, My friend and I) helped the art teacher after school.

6. The secret is between (you and I, you and me).

7. (You and me, You and I) will ride to the game with my mom.

8. Please lend (me, I) an extra pencil.

Rewrite each sentence below, replacing the underlined word or words with a possessive pronoun.

1. Colin needed someone to care for <u>Colin's</u> hamster while he was at camp.

   _____

2. Mr. and Mrs. Williams took home Chinese food for <u>Mr. and Mrs. William's</u> dinner.

   _____

3. The cat washed <u>the cat's</u> tail.

   _____

4. John said, "Dad packed <u>John's</u> favorite lunch, a turkey sandwich."

   _____

5. "Jill, what is <u>Jill's</u> song for <u>Jill's</u> dance in the talent show?"

   _____

6. All the kindergartners brought in <u>the kindergartners'</u> favorite picture books.

   _____

7. Lisa liked to imagine that <u>Lisa's</u> mother could grant every wish.

   _____

8. <u>Ms. Buchanan's</u> class will win the citizenship award for volunteer efforts.

   _____

EXERCISE 33

Rewrite the sentences below, changing the contractions to the correct pairs of words they stand for.

1. He's an amazing athlete!

   _____

2. You'd better not be late for the train, or it will leave without you.

_____

3. We'd brought our film to the photo shop to be developed.

_____

4. She's so fond of horses that she draws them all the time.

_____

5. I'll be sure to call you when I get home.

_____

6. We're going to play kickball at recess.

_____

7. "It's raining cats and dogs" is an idiom that means it's raining heavily.

_____

8. They'll let us rent these videos at a special sale price because they're old.

_____

9. You're the best friend I've ever had!

_____

10. I'm happy that the weekend will be here soon.

_____

EXERCISE 34

Circle the word that correctly completes each sentence.

1. (Your, You're) going to need two sharpened pencils for this test.

2. The printer doesn't work because (its, it's) ink cartridge is empty.

3. (There, Their) is going to be an assembly this afternoon.

4. Do you know if (its, it's) time for us to go to lunch soon?

5. The players changed into (they're, their) uniforms.

6. Please bring (your, you're) smocks to art class.

7. (They're, There) going to repave the street outside school today.

8. (Its, It's) often necessary to take lessons to learn a new skill.

EXERCISE 35

Imagine that you could have dinner with any famous person, living or dead. Which person would you want to have dinner with and why? Write a paragraph below, and be sure to use nouns and pronouns in your response.

_____

_____

_____

_____

_____

_____

_____

_____

EXERCISE 36

Place simple subjects, simple predicates, and pronouns in the correct spaces in the graphic organizers after each sentence below.

1. She bought a blue umbrella.

2. The shoelaces came untied.

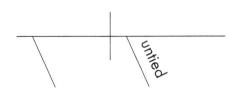

3. Ari gave the absence note to his teacher.

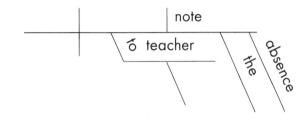

4. Our flag is a symbol of our country.

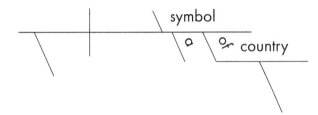

5. Their doctor examined them during their checkups.

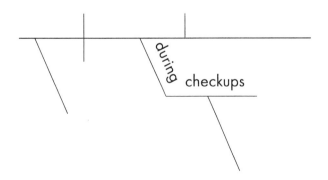

6. Her watch shows the date.

EXERCISE 37

Underline the prepositions in the sentences below. Draw an arrow to their objects.

1. In the United States the Census Bureau's job is to count people.

2. A census is an official counting of the population.

3. Population is the total number of people in a particular place.

4. A population census is taken every ten years in the U.S.

5. During a census, the government polls all of its citizens.

6. Through a census, we can learn many types of data.

7. The name for a scientist who studies population is *demographer*.

8. Demographers get new information from many sources.

9. Demographers learn whether the population in a given place is changing or staying almost the same.

10. Among the data studied are average family size and birthrate.

11. The birthrate of our entire planet is approximately 240,000 a day.

12. Over the last 400 years, world population has increased in the billions.

EXERCISE 38

Collect data about the population in your class. Find out about family size, gender (male or female) of the people living in each home, types of jobs, and types of homes. If you wish, organize your data in bar graphs or pie charts. Then write several paragraphs about your data on a separate piece of paper. Be sure to use prepositional phrases to help provide a clear and accurate picture to the reader.

EXERCISE 39

Complete the diagrams of the sentences below by drawing the rest of the diagram and placing the prepositional phrases in the correct places.

1. The earliest alphabet was developed for written communication.

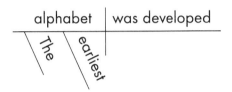

2. Examples of ancient cuneiform writing were discovered in the 1920s.

Examples | were discovered

3. This alphabet was written on clay tablets.

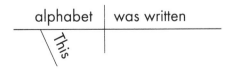

4. Egyptian hieroglyphics influenced the developers of the first alphabet.

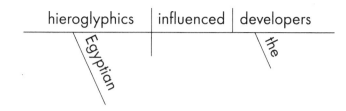

5. This early alphabet came from the Middle East.

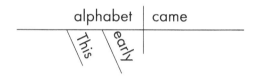

6. This writing system evolved into the Latin alphabet.

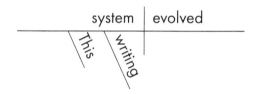

7. People outside this culture developed different alphabets.

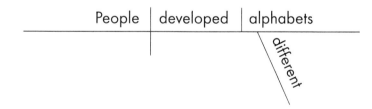

8. Some marks indicate certain vowel sounds in the Hebrew alphabet.

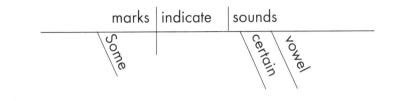

EXERCISE 40

Underline each adjective and draw an arrow to the noun it describes. (Do not underline the articles.) Then place each underlined adjective in the column that tells what kind, which one, or how many.

1. Soil is loose, powdery earth.

2. Most plants grow in soil made up of small pieces of sand, rock, and decayed plant and animal materials.

3. These small pieces of rock were once part of larger rocks.

4. Decayed plants and animal bodies enrich the soil.

5. Through the work of invisible bacteria, the decayed materials create organic material called humus.

6. Earthworms and many kinds of insects help make rich soil.

7. Topsoil is the richest, topmost layer of soil.

8. This soil contains much humus.

9. Underneath the topsoil is a layer of older earth called subsoil.

10. Below all subsoil is bedrock, the deepest layer.

WHAT KIND	WHICH ONE	HOW MANY
_____	_____	_____
_____	_____	_____
_____		_____
_____		
_____		
_____		
_____		
_____		
_____		
_____		
_____		
_____		
_____		

EXERCISE 41

In the blanks, write the correct articles (*a, an, or the*) in the paragraph below.

Milk is _____ important food to many people. _____ farmer is careful about hiring healthy people to handle _____ milk. _____ cows are tested regularly. Once _____ milk is taken from the cows, it is filtered and cooled at _____ milk house. Then it is shipped to _____ milk plant and pumped into large holding tanks. Tests ensure _____ quality and cleanliness of the milk. Pasteurization is _____ process to make milk safe. _____ milk is heated to _____ temperature high enough to kill bacteria. After it is pasteurized, _____ milk is cooled very rapidly. Louis Pasteur, a French scientist, developed _____ process that makes milk as clean and healthy as possible for all the people who drink it.

EXERCISE 42

Underline the correct form of the adjectives in the sentences below.

1. Diamonds are the (harder, hardest) natural substance.

2. On Mohs's scale of minerals, talc is the (soft, softest).

3. Quartz is (hard, harder) than talc, but (softer, softest) than diamonds.

4. Inorganic acids are usually (stronger, strongest) than organic acids.

5. Nitric acid is a (powerful, more powerful) acid.

6. Boric acid is (weak, weaker) than nitric acid.

7. An inch is (short, shorter) than a foot.

8. A yard is (long, longer) than a foot.

9. A mile is the (long, longest) of all.

10. It is (useful, more useful) to be able to compare many types of things.

EXERCISE 43

Write a book review about a story you recently enjoyed. Tell about the setting (time and place), the characters, and the plot. Use as many adjectives as possible.

_____

_____

_____

_____

_____

_____

_____

_____

EXERCISE 44

Read the noun phrases below. Then choose the correct proper adjective from the word bank and rewrite the adjective phrase on the line next to each noun phrase.

ADJECTIVE WORD BANK	NOUN PHRASE	ADJECTIVE PHRASE
Irish	1. leather from Florence	_____
Russian	2. churches in Paris	_____
Chinese	3. soda bread from Ireland	_____
Florentine	4. beef from Texas	_____
Spanish	5. cosmonaut from Russia	_____
Parisian	6. embroidery from China	_____
Texan	7. olives from Greece	_____
Portuguese	8. ceramics from Portugal	_____
Mexican	9. artwork of Spain	_____
Greek	10. vacation in Mexico	_____

EXERCISE 45

Circle the correct form of the irregular adjective in the sentences below.

1. Mr. and Mrs. Williams did a (good, best) job planting flowers in their garden.

2. They thought about planting a Japanese maple tree but decided it would be (better, best) to plant a birch tree instead.

3. Unfortunately, the weather was (bad, worst) on the day they were going to plant it.

4. The next day, the weather was (bad, worse)!

5. After (much, many) days of rain, the weather finally cleared.

6. The Williams had to wait a few (more, most) days for the mud to dry out.

7. The soil had (more, much) water in it than the tree needed.

8. Finally it was a (good, best) time to plant the birch tree.

9. The tree looked so (good, better) that Mr. and Mrs. Williams said they were happy that they waited.

10. Next year they plan to plant (much, many) bushes.

EXERCISE 46

Diagram the following sentences by placing the simple subjects, simple predicates, adjectives, and articles on the proper lines.

1. The stormy weather will end.

2. My mother loves her new red car.

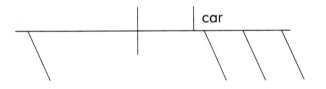

3. Overseas travel is exciting!

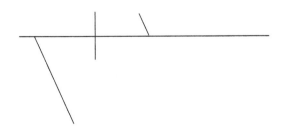

4. Uncle Joe ran a challenging marathon.

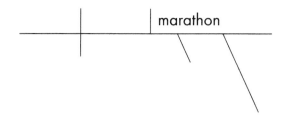

5. Our art museum offers many classes.

EXERCISE 47

Underline each adverb in the sentences below, then draw an arrow from the adverb to the verb it describes.

1. Jill tripped accidentally and knocked over the vase of flowers.

2. Ameesh worked slowly and deliberately.

3. Each contestant played fairly in the contest.

4. Adam's sister will drive soon.

5. I put my pack of gum down and my brother snatched it.

6. Shake hands firmly when you meet someone.

7. Mr. Williams said that everyone did well on the geography test.

8. Let's go on the roller coaster again!

9. Rebecca has lived here all her life.

10. This summer Noel's family will go somewhere they have never been.

EXERCISE 48

Decide whether the adverbs in the sentences below are in the positive, comparative, or superlative form; then write the correct name on the line provided.

1. _____ Colin travels farthest to school.

2. _____ She played the clarinet better than I.

3. _____ The rain fell harder at the beginning of the

storm.

4. _____ She hurried quickly to the car.

5. _____ Samantha arrived earliest for the field trip.

6. _____ The principal spoke softly to the kindergartners.

7. _____ It is important that everyone plays fairly.

8. _____ He solved his students' conflict most skillfully.

EXERCISE 49

Write three sentences using *well* as an adverb that describes a verb.

_____

_____

_____

Write three sentences using *good* as an adjective that describes a noun.

_____

_____

_____

EXERCISE 50

Create graphic organizers and place the simple subjects, simple predicates, and adverbs on the correct lines.

1. Adam ran swiftly.

2. Lisa spells correctly.

3. Rachel hurriedly tied her shoes.

4. Grahame yelled loudly.

5. Javier did not return.

Combine the subjects in the pairs of sentences below using the conjunction *and* to form single sentences with either compound subjects or compound predicates. Write the new sentence on the lines provided.

1. Earthquakes make the earth shake.

   Earthquakes cause the ground to crack.

   _____

   _____

2. The Mercalli scale can measure the effects of earthquakes.

   The Richter scale can measure the effects of earthquakes.

   _____

   _____

3. Poorly constructed buildings are destroyed during a severe earthquake.

   Dams are destroyed during a severe earthquake.

   _____

   _____

4. Earthquake-proof buildings must have foundations built into solid rock.

   Earthquake-proof buildings must be able to move without shattering.

   _____

   _____

5. Scientists continuously monitor earthquakes.

   Scientists plot the sites of major quakes on a map.

   _____

   _____

6. The epicenter, the earthquake source, can be plotted.

   The hypocenter, the source of the shock waves, can be plotted.

   _____

   _____

7. Shock waves extend from the earthquake's center.

Shock waves move in several different patterns.

_____

_____

EXERCISE 52

Use the conjunction given to combine each pair of related sentences into a compound sentence. Rewrite the sentences on the lines. Do not forget to place a comma before the conjunction.

1. and   The chinook is a warm, dry wind. It is caused by air that flows down the sides of mountains.

_____

_____

2. and   Hot air expands. The change produces a sound we know as thunder.

_____

_____

3. but   Tropical storms along the eastern U.S. are called hurricanes. In the northwest Pacific they are called typhoons.

_____

_____

4. or   In a severe hurricane, families can move to special shelters nearby. They can leave the area.

_____

_____

5. so   Many people need help evacuating before a storm. Organizations such as the Red Cross try to help.

_____

_____

6. and   Tornadoes can cause terrible destruction. There is no way to lessen their effects.

_____

_____

7. or   You might see sheet lightning during a storm. You could see forked lightning.

_____

_____

8. so   Big clouds cause heavy rain. Get into shelter when you see them.

_____

_____

EXERCISE 53

Describe a recent event in your school or community, such as a parade, a sports game, or a concert. Make sure to use some compound sentences in place of short, related ones.

_____

_____

_____

_____

_____

_____

_____

_____

_____

_____

_____

_____

_____

EXERCISE 54

Expand the following sentences by adding appositives, prepositional phrases, adjectives, and adverbs.

1. Sand is blowing.

   _____

2. Natural resources are important.

   _____

3. Fish breathe.

   _____

4. Plants bloom.

   _____

5. The rock band played.

   _____

Complete the diagrams below by placing the missing parts correctly on the graphic organizers.

1. Police officers and firefighters help citizens in difficulty.

2. Police keep order and direct traffic.

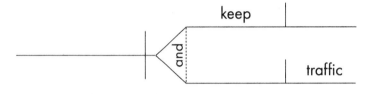

3. Firefighters stop fires, and they educate the community.

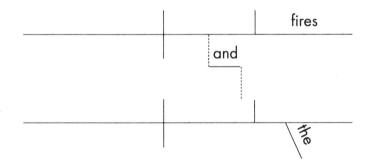

4. Police patrol in cars with special markings.

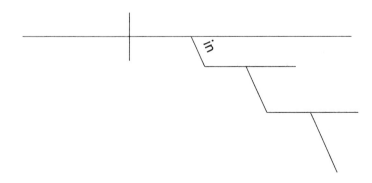

RIDGEWOOD GRAMMAR

5. Firefighters arrive quickly in emergencies.

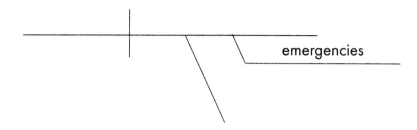